The
COMPOSITE
OF THE
WOMAN

Her Distinction in Kind

Sharon R. Peters, PhD

ISBN 978-1-64515-818-9 (paperback)
ISBN 978-1-64515-819-6 (digital)

Christian Faith Publishing, Inc.
832 Park Avenue
Meadville, PA 16335
www.christianfaithpublishing.com

Printed in the United States of America

To my one and only "biological daughter," Shaniece Dakira Ruff. May she find herself within the pages of this book. It is my earnest prayer that my own daughter (whom I conceived and birthed) finds the measure of grace she needs to be the awesome woman of faith that God wonderfully made her to be, for she is a twenty-first-century Esther, a queen (in her own right) called for "such a time as this." I love you, Shaniece!

FOREWORD
by
Dr. Ramona Joseph

What a marvelous read, **The Composite of the Woman, Her Distinction in Kind** by Dr. Sharon R. Peters captures every woman that is "not every woman" with definitions that are theologically sound, but 21st Century relative. My spiritual daughter has done her homework to present an in-depth study of many notable women from the Bible. In addition, she has tempered her writing not to be **religious but spiritual to give insight to all women are and are not, as God used them to be effective** and to affect the dynamics of the lives of the people they touched.

The 21st Century woman is the CREATION of God with an image and purpose she can manifest whether sinner or fallen because there is redemption for her. The CREATION of God, **The Composite of The Woman**, must be the image and likeness of God through her purpose of virtue, wisdom, unmarried, married, working and as a leader. Dr. Peters challenges women, through this dynamic book, to see all the composites and to hold them up to the mirror of their own lives. In that mirror, they are given examples and options to change, become good, better and the best.

As the reader moves to different dimensions of that entire woman God has created; His "spirituality" to be in the earth realm, **The Composite of The Woman, Her Distinction in Kind,** is a must to be read and re-read as self-help for improvement.

Continue to challenge women, Dr. Sharon Peters, my beloved spiritual daughter. Your written word is meaningful as readers assimilate the divine knowledge God has given you.

Love and peace
Dr. Mom+

CONTENTS

Acknowledgments 9

Preface..11

Chapter 1:   Woman in the Beginning 13

Chapter 2:   The Fallen Woman 17

Chapter 3:   The Virtuous Woman 21

Chapter 4:   The Strange Woman 24

Chapter 5:   The Silly Woman 29

Chapter 6:   The Foolish Woman 31

Chapter 7:   The Wise Woman 35

Chapter 8:   The Appointed Woman 39

Chapter 9:   The Blessed and Highly Favored Woman.................42

Chapter 10: The Leading Woman 44

Chapter 11: The Saved Woman 50

Chapter 12: The Sinner Woman...52

Chapter 13: The Worshipping Woman................................55

Chapter 14: The Married Woman 60

Chapter 15: The Unmarried Woman...................................63

Chapter 16: The Barren Woman 66

Chapter 17: The Free Woman 71

Chapter 18: The Bondwoman 74

Chapter 19: The Desolate Woman 78

Chapter 20: The Working Woman 82

Chapter 21: The Troubled Woman......................................87

The Conclusion 91

ACKNOWLEDGMENTS

First, I can't help but to acknowledge my Lord and my Savior, Jesus Christ, the personhood of the Son of God, whom Elohim the Creator of all sent into the earth to purchase back my soul with his blood! Second, I acknowledge my husband, Apostle Robbie C. Peters, whom I love. Third, I acknowledge my mother and my father, Marion and Janet Stringer for (void of them) coming together, there would be "no me" in the earth. Fourthly, I acknowledge my biological children, Shaniece and Kyle Ruff, and my bonus children who God has blessed to be blended into my life, DeJuan, Isaiah, Lyric, and Nina Peters. Then there's Shaniya Burnett, my grandchild who is my prototype (me in originality).

I acknowledge my many spiritual daughters and the countless women from all walks of life who have allowed me to "spiritually mother" them, lead them, mentor them, or direct them into their purpose, calling, or destiny in some way.

I acknowledge two seasoned women of great faith who spiritually mothered me while greatly impacting my life with wisdom; Pastor Emeritus Joyce A. Harper and Dr. Ramona Joseph. Finally, I acknowledge my brother and friend, Prophet John Veal, who prophesied this book many years ago by seeing it and saying to me, "I see the title of the book, but I cannot interpret its meaning." Truly, this book is the Lord's doing, and it is marvelous in our eyes!

ACKNOWLEDGMENTS

PREFACE

Being called to minister (serve) women and having a purpose that entails being "a standard of holiness for women," I have had the awesome privilege of reaching and engaging with a host of women for many years. In addition, I would like to think, since I'm used by God to help, aid, counsel, strengthen, train, mentor, teach, affirm, and empower women from all walks of life, as well as be "an example" to them and a "model" for them, I think I can say I know something about the woman in kind. Therefore, I say with certainty that *no one woman is the same*. We (the WOMAN), are all the same gender (i.e. female) yet the "kind" of woman that we are varies from woman to woman as we present ourselves through our womanhood. It is a dangerous thing to group all women in one barrel and stereotype us all into one class. This would be a huge mistake and would steer one away from understanding the WOMAN or properly recognizing the WOMAN in her diversity of kind or composite. Yet, this is exactly what many do or how they define the woman in speech.

This book is designed to segment the WOMAN as a compositional reading showing forth her divine qualities and bringing some recognition to the makeup of "disparate" or separate parts of the WOMAN in identity that are not of God yet have become (through experience or choice) a part of her make-up in kind. It is my prayer that the woman reading this book will find her "true identity" in specific and in composite. Then, I pray that the man who is brave enough to pick up this book and read it will see that every woman is not the same, for truly we vary in kind. I hope that everyone reading this book will start to see and understand that there are "influencers" to our womanhood or manhood (for that matter) that was not us in originality or in creation. I truly believe God wants these things exposed so that they can be purged from our womanhood ladies and so that we can truly exemplify the WOMAN that is of God and not a false woman in our presentation to men, our children and any other human forms that we relate to daily. So, journey along with me as I unveil the WOMAN in composite as well as her distinction in kind.

CHAPTER 1

Woman in the Beginning

So God created man in his own image, in the image of
God created he him; male and female created he them.
—Genesis 1:27

W OMAN in the beginning was a "female" who was created by God
(in spirit) at the same time he created the "male" version of mankind.
Again, the male and the female were both created in spirit by God
at the same time! Listen to what God said to His Triune Being (The
Father, Son, and The Holy Spirit) concerning the creation of mankind.

> Then God said, "Let us make *mankind* in
> our image, in our likeness, so that (they) may rule
> over the fish in the sea and the birds in the sky,
> over the livestock and all the wild animals, and
> over all the creatures that move along the ground.
> (Genesis 1:26, NIV)

Scripture highlights that God's original plan for mankind (which
had two kinds, i.e. male and female) was that they *both* would have rule
and dominion over every living thing in the earth. So we can say in the
beginning that male and the female had equal rule in the earth! They
(male and female) had *dual dominion* in the earth; please remember this
as you read the next chapter where I talk about the FALLEN WOMAN!

WOMAN in the beginning was a "female" with equal spiritual authority in the earth (along with her "male" partner in spirit). Therefore, it is scripturally safe and sound to say that God *never* intended for a man to lord over a woman. Then why does this happen so much, you may ask? The answer: *the fall of mankind* altered God's plan for mankind! Again, we will discuss more about this in the next chapter, but for now allow me to continue to talk about the WOMAN in the beginning.

Now, the word WOMAN was first mentioned by God when he saw purpose in bringing her forth as a helpmeet for Adam. I recommend you, Woman, read my book *Help for the Help Meet* to gain further specific insight on the woman who is a man's wife/helpmeet. Listen to the scriptures:

> And the rib, which the Lord God had taken
> from man, made he a woman, and brought her
> unto the man. (Genesis 2:22)

God made a woman from the man's rib, and when God brought or presented her to the man, he recognized her first as someone who was part of him (that's partnership in creation). Secondly, he had the intellect or divine knowing to call her (the woman) exactly what God had made or created. This is key, Woman, to your identity!

Never allow yourself to be "called or named" anything less or opposite of your divine created being. Who you were created to be should be the composite or distinction of your being and woman, you must realize that God didn't make anything that was junk, trash, or unusable in purpose! Woman, you too are among all the other things that God himself defined as *good*! Therefore, we can say if a man finds a woman who is "wife-matured," then he has found *a good thing*, so says Proverbs 18:22. Adam recognized the WOMAN (as a good thing) created by God and fashioned to be his wife an equal partner in the earth!

FEMALE is her spiritual birth name, which God called her in the beginning and WOMAN is her natural birth name, which God said he would make and Adam named or correctly called her when God presented her to him.

Listen to what Adam said: "And Adam said, This is now bone of my bones, and flesh of my flesh: she shall be called Woman, because she was taken out of Man" (Genesis 2:23). Now this knowing requires a Selah or a (pause and think on this moment) because, although God allowed Adam to name the animals and the FEMALE, we as women must be very careful about allowing "ill advised" men to name us, and you must *never* allow anyone to call you out of your name. Why? Because names correspond to identity, and names shape our identity too. Names also speak to our nature and our makeup, as well as our doings.

Note: Woman, your title does not make you in identity, but *your name does*! Listen to what the Bible says about a name:

A good name is rather to be chosen than
great riches, and loving favour rather than silver
and gold. (Proverbs 22:1)

Woman, your name should be chosen and should not be used as some "label" to put on you because of "bad choices" or due to your mistakes which you can successfully "live past." To God be the Glory! Woman, you cannot allow "worldly names" to be placed upon you to degrade or put you down as some "worthless" creation of God, because that is not who you were created or were built to be. Before I continue, listed below are some of the negative names of women which I would like *to curse right now* in Jesus's name, for they have no connection to your divine identity or your womanhood!

Keep in mind, every culture or ethnic group has degrading names for women, so as you are reading this book, you might want to take the time to "recall" these names and then curse every foul name your culture calls women, as I curse the ones I know and have heard women referred to as.

- Bust Down
- Runner
- Hood Rat
- Bit-h

- Cow or Heifer
- Wifey (makes worldly *the wife factor*)
- Baby Mama (this one is universal)
- Hag
- Welfare Queen
- Jezebel (demeans *the leading lady*)
- Witch
- Dike
- Slut
- Cunt
- Whore
- Hussy
- Ratchet

And all the like, I *curse* these names, for they played no part in our creation as WOMAN. None of these "names" were used in creation to define the WOMAN!

Let us pray.

> Father, I thank you that you called the woman "female" in originality and you allowed Adam to name the first WOMAN you formed and built because you had endowed him with intellect and you trusted his wisdom to recognize your creation and the compatible part of himself! Therefore, Father, I curse every name that the woman has been called not to purposely *name her but to label her* with an evil connotation of her being! I curse these influencers of her womanhood! I curse the "negative effects" that these names has had on her life like low self-esteem and dimensioned self-worth and value! Right now, Father, reverse the stigma that these names have had on the female gender and start the rebuilding process of the WOMAN now, in Jesus's name, I pray. Amen!

CHAPTER 2

The Fallen Woman

And the serpent said unto the woman, Ye shall not surely die:
For God doth know that in the day ye eat thereof, then your
eyes shall be opened, and ye shall be as gods, knowing good
and evil. And when the woman saw that the tree was good
for food, and that it was pleasant to the eyes, and a tree to be
desired to make one wise, she took of the fruit thereof, and did
eat, and gave also unto her husband with her; and he did eat.

—Genesis 3:4–6

I am often summoned or invited to preach or speak at women's services, retreats, conferences, etc. In these services, I was sent by God
to encourage or uplift women, even esteem them back to the place of
their origin or place in God. I have addressed many issues that plague
women in purposeful counsel, utilizing the word of God as a tool to
bring healing and deliverance to women everywhere.

I was asked one time to minister at a church's Annual Women's
Weekend, and their theme was: "Women Repositioning Ourselves
Back to our Original Place in God"! Well, the Lord gave me an
interesting word to expound on, and it was entitled "The Falling
Woman"! It is in this chapter that I want to address her in recogni-
tion because she appears in the Bible right after creation and Eden
Living. It is this woman who Adam blamed for his spiritual fall in the
garden, so she warrants being examined in character to prevent you,

WOMAN, from likewise falling at the hands of the serpent's "beguilement," which is also deception!

The FALLING WOMAN has desires that are not of God, and it is "that woman" that the devil seeks to beguile or deceive! The first woman was made a GOOD WOMAN but "desired" the tree that was in the midst of the garden which God had forbidden. She saw it to be good for food, and I say everything that is good is not necessarily GOD or "God-ordained." What you desire, woman, can signal to Satan the direction in which you are leaning, so you, woman, must *watch your desires*! Woman, *again,* what you desire may be signaling to the devil that you are "leaning and bending" towards your own iniquity (which is your own inclination towards evil or your "sin choice" or preference) and this WOMAN is in you! However, good news, WOMAN, the Bible says in Psalm 16:6 that by "mercy and truth," iniquity is purged (that is, out of you, Woman). Thank God that He is merciful and His word is true.

Now listen to what Lucifer said in the Bible before his fall. Hear his desire as mentioned by the Prophet Isaiah's report of this in Isaiah 14:12–14. "How art thou fallen from heaven, O Lucifer, son of the morning! how art thou cut down to the ground, which didst weaken the nations! For thou hast said in thine heart, I will ascend into heaven, I will exalt my throne above the stars of God: I will sit also upon the mount of the congregation, in the sides of the north: I will ascend above the heights of the clouds; I will be like the most High."

You see, "Lucifer is falling" simply by the "ungodly" expression of his will, which is not God's will for him. Likewise, Woman, your will may not be I AM's will for your life, and you are a "falling woman" when your desires supersede God's will, because your falling in nature is being exhibited by your expressed will or desires which, again, is not divine. You must desire what God desires for your life, and any other desire obtained will be a "willful fall." I pray you can see this.

When you don't desire what God wants for your life, you need to get to Gethsemane (i.e. in a place of prayer) where the oil can be pressed out of you so you can do the will of the Father. This is what

Jesus did when His soul was rejecting the will of God because he did not desire to drink the "bitter cup" of the cross. If you don't get to Gethsemane, then you will be just like Eve. You will eventually succumb to your own will, moving you from a FALLING WOMAN to a FALLEN WOMAN! You must not allow a fallen nature to cause you to be deceived by the devil and partake in that which God has given instruction in His word or specifics to you not to partake in!

Please remember this: A "fallen woman" is a woman who is out of fellowship with God. This woman has allowed her nature to take her down and away from God. She like the FIRST WOMAN, Eve, is listening and conversing about things which God has forbidden for her life! What's the point of talking about that which God has forbidden for your life, woman? *The forbidden is not up for discussion!*

Now listen to what God said to "the fallen woman" in the Garden of Eden.

> Unto the woman he said, "I will greatly multiply thy sorrow and thy conception; in sorrow thou shalt bring forth children; and thy desire shall be to thy husband, and he shall rule over thee." (Genesis 3:16)

"Multiplied sorrows" is what the fallen woman can expect if she does not allow Jesus Christ to redeem her from the penalty of her sin, and if she does not allow the Spirit of God to regenerate her by renewing her spirit through a born-again experience. In addition, it was the fallen woman who altered her desire away from God's rule, and it was the fallen woman whose husband would now *rule her*! This was not the original plan of God that the man would "rule" over the woman, but that they would have *equal rulership* and *dominion* in the earth as was stated in chapter one. The fall of the woman altered her affection and her position in the earth! However, thanks be unto God, Jesus, through salvation and our personal relationship with Him, repositioned the WOMAN, and Jesus gave us our "positional authority" back, which we had in the beginning! Therefore, if you are a "falling" or FALLEN WOMAN, and you recognize the error of your nature *now* by reading this chapter, rather than let your "old man" or a degenerate nature take you further and further away from the Father, my prayer is that you recognize this first, WOMAN: Repositioning and restoration requires *repentance first!*

CHAPTER 3

The Virtuous Woman

Who can find a virtuous woman? for her price is far above rubies.
—Proverbs 31:10

The Proverbs 31 Woman (the Virtuous Woman) has been preached and expounded upon at Women's Day services all around the globe! God knows I have preached at hundreds of these services with the theme of the day coming from this scripture reference. However, one Mother's Day, the Lord gave me a revelation on "The Virtuous Woman" that was so profound and caused me to convey this woman in a way that I knew my audience had *never* heard before. So please allow me to share her and the revelation about her with you in this chapter.

The Virtuous Woman in revelatory enlightenment, shows us the primary concerns of the virtuous woman, which is her husband's well-being and/or her household's well-being which, of course, includes her children. In addition, if I had to state a third area of concern of the virtuous woman, it would be her concern for those who are less fortunate or those in need. This is the marking of the virtuous woman. Again, she cares for her husband and/or her household with the strength of her hands, which God empowers by way of her *virtue*! As a sidebar (which I will not go into any further than this in this book), the woman mentioned in Proverbs 31 is a depiction of "the church," or we can say, "The Bride of Christ." Let's continue.

What does it mean to be virtuous?

Virtuous, defined in Dictionary.com, is conforming to moral and ethical principles or morally Excellent; upright.

The Virtuous Woman is a *woman of integrity*! She's a CHASTE WOMAN! Now listen to the Hebrew translation of "virtuous" to hear some great revelation and see how it sounds like the church universal!

Virtuous in Hebrew is *chayil*, which means "probably *a force*" whether by means or other resources (which the virtuous woman has); so we can say "the virtuous woman is a force to be reckoned with."

The CHAYIL WOMAN has:

An army, wealth (which means more than money), virtue, valor, and strength!

The Virtuous Woman is *able*, and she has *abilities*! Therefore, the king's mother taught him as he mentioned this in Proverbs. "Who can find her for her price is far above rubies"! In other words, The Virtuous Woman is likened unto a very "pricey" rare jewel which is very hard to find. Men find wives, but the Holy Ghost finds the Virtuous Woman because she's very difficult to find, and a man will need the help of the Holy Spirit to lead him to her.

The *Chayil* or Virtuous Woman, according to Hebrew translation, is *active*. Not a busybody, but she is *active*, and she has "a company" with her that resembles a great force!

A *Chayil* or Virtuous Woman has goods of her own! She is not labeled a "gold digger," again, as some women are labeled, because this woman pursues men for the "things" he can give her, never acquiring anything on her own or with her own hands, which we will see that the Virtuous Woman does. She has *substance* too, due to the labor she does with, again, *her own hands*. This woman has might, power, riches, and strength.

Lastly, the CHAYIL WOMAN has a fully loaded train; she is vigilant and she is "war ready!" So when we break down the composite of the Virtuous Woman or the CHAYIL WOMAN, we can now see why the value of her worth is far above rubies as the Bible says!

So if you are this woman (and you know it), please don't ever allow any man or person to devalue you or lessen your worth. You must understand the quality and the wealth of your virtue and remain a cut above the rest, being assured that everything you put your "hands" to will prosper! By the way, go now and look at Proverbs 31 and read about all "The Virtuous Woman" did with her hands, then go work with your own hands, CHAYIL WOMAN, for truly, you will be given the fruit of your hands.

Always remember, woman, *your hands* can be used for more than a show piece of "gel nails" and pretty "no chip polish," because your hands, used as a *woman of virtue*, can work a good work in your home, community, the marketplace, and the kingdom.

CHAPTER 4

The Strange Woman

For the lips of a "strange woman" drop as an honeycomb,
and her mouth is smoother than oil: But her end is
bitter as wormwood, sharp as a two-edged sword. Her
feet go down to death; her steps take hold on hell.
—Proverbs 5:3–5

The Strange Woman is a very evil woman. She is a woman who will experience the death of her purpose, and she is a woman whose own feet will place her in hell, so says the scriptures. Rarely is the Strange Woman discussed and identified, yet wisdom spots her quite easily, for she is the woman with the flattering mouth! Flattery is often deceptive and is used to lure her prey into her web of destruction. The above scripture says her mouth is smoother than oil. A more modern-day depiction of the Strange Woman would be that she is a very "slick woman." This is the kind or type of woman that the Bible instructs a man to stay away from. Listen to the Word of God: "Remove thy way far from her, and come not nigh the door of her house" (Proverbs 5:8).

Although the Bible speaks explicitly and warns "sons" about the danger of the Strange Woman, sadly this is the WOMAN that many men (of the falling kind) seem to lust after, for even the scripture speaks against them doing. Let's review:

> To keep thee from the evil woman, from the flattery of the tongue of "a strange woman." Lust not after her beauty in thine heart; neither let her take thee with her eyelids. For by means of a "whorish woman" a man is brought to a piece of bread: and the adultress will hunt for the precious life. Can a man take fire in his bosom, and his clothes not be burned? Can one go upon hot coals, and his feet not be burned? (Proverbs 6:24–28)

The Strange Woman, as we can see from this passage of scripture, is a very "seductive woman," and she uses her beauty and her feminine gestures to seduce her prey. The result of the Strange Woman's tactics is to cause the fall of the man who involves himself with her. Here, the scriptures liken The Strange Woman to a "whorish woman" and an "adulteress," which is not a woman you should ever aspire to be, although there are many women who bear the characteristics of The Strange Woman.

Again, if we look further at the Proverbs, we will see that scriptures written about the Strange Woman were words of wisdom being given to sons concerning this woman. Let's review chapter seven to learn more about this kind of woman who has caused the death of the character, integrity even the ministry, of many male preachers and the careers of politicians, athletes, even men in general, and especially men in high positions of authority.

> My son, keep my words, and lay up my commandments with thee. That they may keep thee from "the strange woman," from the stranger which flattereth with her words. For at the window of my house I looked through my casement, And beheld among the simple ones, I discerned

among the youths, a young man void of understanding, Passing through the street near her corner; and he went the way to her house, In the twi-
light, in the evening, in the black and dark night:
And, behold, there met him "a woman with the
attire of an harlot," and "subtil of heart." ("She
is loud and stubborn"; her feet abide not in her
house: Now is she without, now in the streets,
and lieth in wait at every corner.) So she caught
him, and kissed him, and with an impudent face
said unto him, I have peace offerings with me;
this day have I payed my vows. Therefore came
I forth to meet thee, diligently to seek thy face,
and I have found thee. I have decked my bed
with coverings of tapestry, with carved works,
with fine linen of Egypt. I have perfumed my
bed with myrrh, aloes, and cinnamon. Come, let
us take our fill of love until the morning: let us
solace ourselves with loves. For the goodman is
not at home, he is gone a long journey: He hath
taken a bag of money with him, and will come
home at the day appointed. With her much fair
speech she caused him to yield, with the flattering of her lips she forced him. He goeth after
her straightway, as an ox goeth to the slaughter,
or as a fool to the correction of the stocks; Till
a dart strike through his liver; as a bird hasteth
to the snare, and knoweth not that it is for his
life. Hearken unto me now therefore, O ye children, and attend to the words of my mouth.
Let not thine heart decline to her ways, go not
astray in her paths. For she hath cast down many
wounded: yea, many strong men have been slain
by her. Her house is the way to hell, going down
to the chambers of death. (Proverbs 7:1, 5–27)

As you can see, the "scent" of the Strange Woman" leaks with *lust*! The aroma she projects is not a sweet aroma of godliness, for she is not "sweetly saved," but she is lustfully endowed in a spiritual smell that is not godly. She's an easy "bedmate" and quite alluring with her flattering words! Truly, there is a difference, WOMAN, between affirming with words and flattering with words. Flattery is excessive "insincere" praise, done with speech or words, that's very strange in nature. Excessive compliments always felt strange, even agitating, to me and often made me want to rebuke the person doing it like the Apostle Paul did that little girl with the spirit of divination in Acts chapter sixteen.

The Strange Woman, with her clamorous loudness, is lethal to the destiny of a man. The most she can offer a man is death to his assignment, mandate, ministry, and his marriage, and please know the Strange Woman is "hell sent" and is a woman on assignment to destroy any man that falls prey to her snare and trap. Woman, please know this—you were created by God to be a "suitable" companion to a man, and nothing about your identity should be strange. As a matter of truth, your suitability should be quite recognizable to him.

Lastly, allow me to address your dress attire, woman, by way of this chapter. Please pay attention to the way you dress so that you will not be likened unto the Strange Woman simply due to your dress attire. Note the scripture above in Proverbs. Chapter seven said she (the Strange Woman) is a woman with "the attire of a harlot" or prostitute, and she is subtle (or crafty) in heart. To the WOMAN reading this chapter, allow me to ask you this: What's in your heart when you pick out or choose your dress attire? I've heard many women say they consult with God about what to put on. Well, I would venture to say I do believe every woman should assess why she wears what she wears. Do you use clothes to attract or allure? Do you wear what you wear to identify with the world or Hollywood? The harlot or the prostitute dresses to allure or attract her customer. Likewise, the Strange Woman has a purpose for the way she dresses. If you dress in attire to allure or distract those that look upon you, then more than likely, you are leaning towards being a strange woman, which is in no way godly in nature. Truly, I believe a woman can make a fashion statement *without* being alluring or distracting in her attire. Different is okay, but being THE STRANGE WOMAN is a cause for concern. Please *do not* be THE STRANGE WOMAN, for if you are her (in kind), then you need deliverance. *Get it quickly* before the likes of her lead you to a place you will regret being in later. I will be praying for you.

CHAPTER 5

The Silly Woman

For of this sort are they which creep into houses, and lead captive
silly women laden with sins, led away with divers lusts, Ever
learning, and never able to come to the knowledge of the truth.
—2 Timothy 3:6–7

According to Paul's writing here in 2 Timothy chapter 4, silly
women will be a part of the perilous (or dangerous) phenomenon that
we will see in the last day. So you should expect a rise in silly women
as the last days unfold before us. Paul lets us know that men will be
lovers of themselves (meaning they won't love you, woman, and they
won't love God), children will be disobedient to their parents, and
you're going to see the Silly Woman everywhere. This woman will
be in your church, on your block, in the cubicle next to you on your
job; she will be in a myriad of places!

Paul said it is the Silly Woman that people, having "forms of
godliness" and denying the power thereof, will go after! It is the Silly
Woman that will be lead captive in the last day, for she will be ever
learning and *never* coming into the knowledge of truth. This also
lets us know that the Silly Woman is void of knowledge that is true
knowledge. In other words, what this woman is learning *is not truth*.

The Silly Woman is laden with sin! In other words, she is "loaded"
with sin, and they have piled up in her life. If this is you, woman, I
beseech you to *repent now,* for Jesus Christ is just the person for this man-

ner of woman. If you humble yourself and go low, the Lord will forgive you of your sins and cleanse you of all your unrighteousness, woman!

The Silly Woman is a woman with various kinds of lustful desires. The Silly Woman has a "manifold" lust problem, and it's wrapped all up in her character even. If this is you, woman, again you need Jesus to deliver you from your sinful nature! You, woman, need to be washed with the water of the word thus sanctifying you in nature. If lust is a part of your nature, woman, you are a candidate for deliverance! You need to be freed from your captivity! Listen to what Jesus said about His "anointed ministry" in Luke chapter 4.

> The Spirit of the Lord is upon me, because he hath anointed me to preach the gospel to the poor; he hath sent me to heal the brokenhearted, to *preach deliverance to the captives*, and recovering of sight to the blind, to set at liberty them that are bruised, to preach the acceptable year of the Lord. (Luke 4:18–19)

Woman, if you fit the character or portray the likings of the Silly Woman, you need to sit in a local church assembly where deliverance is preached and executed! You need the Word of God, Woman. Be aware that forms of godliness have no *power,* and those with godly forms are coming for you, and they will put you in captivity with no key to set you free. Therefore, I advise you, woman, to hide yourself in a word-based church so that you may come into the knowledge of truth; for it is the word and the truth that brings the power to set you free! Plus, it takes someone with an anointing to destroy the yoke that has you in captivity. Again, I say unto you, The Silly Woman is a target for ungodly men, they are coming after you woman and they will put *you*, THE SILLY WOMAN, *in bondage*! However, the ministry and anointing of Christ will cause you to be delivered and free (at liberty), for whom the Son sets free is *free indeed*!

> If the Son therefore shall make you free, ye shall be free indeed. (John 8:36)

CHAPTER 6

The Foolish Woman

A foolish woman is clamorous: she is simple, and knoweth nothing.
—Proverbs 9:13

Foolish is something that no woman should ever desire to be. The above scripture describes some key character traits of the Foolish Woman!

- She's clamorous (or loud)!
- She's simple (or lacking mental acuteness)!
- She knows nothing (i.e. void of knowledge)!

This is horrible and should not be the case with any woman! The Foolish Woman does not do good at building her home either, for the scripture says she plucks it down with her hands! (See Proverbs 14:1.)

Foolish people are always opening their mouths and speaking what they do not know or what they have no knowledge of or what their finite minds cannot even understand! Job's wife spoke like a Foolish Woman when she looked at him suffering physically due to the illness that struck his body, and she told him to "curse God and die." Let's review this in Job chapter 2:

> So went Satan forth from the presence of
> the Lord, and smote Job with sore boils from the

sole of his foot unto his crown. And he took him a potsherd to scrape himself withal; and he sat down among the ashes. Then said his wife unto him, Dost thou still retain thine integrity? curse God, and die. But he said unto her, "Thou speakest as one of the foolish women speaketh." What? shall we receive good at the hand of God, and shall we not receive evil? In all this did not Job sin with his lips. (Job 2:7–10)

I think we all will agree that what Job's wife suggested to her "upright husband" to do was void of wisdom, not to mention it was not very supportive to her husband while he was in his trial. As a result, to Job, she spoke as one of the Foolish Women as he told her. Therefore, we can go on to say that "the Foolish Woman" is insensitive in speech and allows just about anything to come out of her mouth! Of course, she's the opposite of the wise woman who governs her mouth with wisdom and administers grace with words. We will examine the wise woman in the next chapter. However, worst yet, the Foolish Woman who takes her character from THE FOOL who speaks irreverently *about God,* not just out loud, but also in their heart! Hear the Word:

The fool hath said in his heart, There is no God. They are corrupt, they have done abominable works, there is none that doeth good. (Psalm 14:1)

Also, according to this scripture, *fools can do no good!* Conversely, woman, you were deemed *to be good* by God in creation, so why would you take on the character of *a fool* thus lessening or devaluing the very essence of your creation? Please don't be a foolish woman!

Now another thing about foolishness. According to Proverbs 26:11, foolishness has a repeat cycle, for it's something that the Foolish Woman reverts to. Hear the word: "As a dog returns to its vomit, so a fool repeats his foolishness" (Proverbs 26:11, NLT). In other words, *fools are repeat offenders* for, again, they often revert to their foolish ways!

For my last discourse, allow me to show you something else about the Foolish Woman in my attempt to steer you away from her practices in character, for the Word of God uses her in description to teach us a kingdom principle. That being the importance of *being prepared* for the things of God, like the return of Jesus Christ, for instance. It's foolish to not prepare for His coming! Let's review a passage of scripture in Matthew chapter twenty-five.

> Then shall the kingdom of heaven be likened unto ten virgins, which took their lamps, and went forth to meet the bridegroom. And five of them were wise, and five were foolish. They that were foolish took their lamps, and took no oil with them: But the wise took oil in their vessels with their lamps. While the bridegroom tarried, they all slumbered and slept. And at midnight there was a cry made, Behold, the bridegroom cometh; go ye out to meet him. Then all those virgins arose, and trimmed their lamps. And the foolish said unto the wise, Give us of your oil; for our lamps are gone out. But the wise answered, saying, Not so; lest there be not enough for us and you: but go ye rather to them that sell, and buy for yourselves. And while they went to buy, the bridegroom came; and they that were ready went in with him to the marriage: and the door was shut. (Matthew 25:1–10)

The Foolish Woman is an "unprepared woman." She's not prepared for where she's going, yet she still tries to go only to have doors slam in her face. Her foolish practices keep her outside the doors of opportunity. The Foolish Woman is lacking in preparation for where she's trying to go. Keep in mind, the scripture says the foolish virgins took their lamps, but they took no oil with them—that was foolish.

If I was preaching, I would tell you to write this down: *light and oil go together*, pause, and think on this. Listen, if you have ever lit a candle after it burns for a while, what you will start to see is the formation of *oil*. Go try it! *This is quite powerful!*

Let me close out this chapter with this: The Foolish Woman can never exemplify the true anointing of Christ in her life because she has allowed the light of Christ to go out in her life. So please don't be a foolish woman; keep the light on, let the oil burn, and *always* prepare for where God would have you to go!

CHAPTER 7

The Wise Woman

> Every wise woman buildeth her house: but the
> foolish plucketh it down with her hands.
>
> —Proverbs 14:1

The Wise Woman is a master builder, among other things. It takes wisdom to be a *builder*, for builders must understand the blueprint, for it highlights the design of that which is being built. Builders must have knowledgeable understanding of the purpose of what is being built. I like to say that wisdom is knowledge guided by understanding. Listen to what the Bible says about wisdom:

> Wisdom is the principal thing; therefore get wisdom: and with all thy getting get understanding. Exalt her, and she shall promote thee: she shall bring thee to honour, when thou dost embrace her. She shall give to thine head an ornament of grace: a crown of glory shall she deliver to thee. (Proverbs 4:7–9)

Wisdom sounds like a "feminine" person, since the Bible refers to wisdom as a "her or a she" in this passage of scripture six times. I will venture to say then that godly wisdom is the "feminine side" of God. Godly wisdom, metaphorically speaking, is "The First Lady" of heaven; she's the principal thing! In other words, wisdom is *first* in rank, chief, and the beginning. Wisdom is not what you seek after the fact or after all else has failed you! You need wisdom to rank *first* in your life in terms of character. You, woman, need to be endowed with wisdom and you don't need to be "lacking" in wisdom especially if you are trying to *build*. Godly wisdom gives you the right (or divine) perspective of a matter, and when you look through the lens of wisdom, you see things right or godly, which causes you to understand more clearly. Wisdom brings with it honor, promotion, wealth, and riches. Wisdom, when exalted to a first position in your life, will bring with it "a *crown* of glory" which you, woman, will get to gracefully wear!

Now let's look at the character of the Wise Woman by reviewing a biblical woman named Abigail as highlighted in 1 Samuel 25. The scripture starts off defining Abigail as *a woman of understanding*, which is a marking of the Wise Woman. This woman has gotten some understanding, for the Bible says with all thy getting, *get understanding!* Again, wisdom breeds understanding. So Abigail, we can say, was a "wise woman" who was married to a man named "Nabal," whose name means "stupid, wicked, or foolish." Abigail (if you continue reading in the scriptures) had a response to her husband's (unwise) response to the king's request for food that exemplified wisdom coupled with intercession which, by the way, is a powerful combination. You can clearly see that this woman had understanding in how to reverse the consequences (which intercession often does) of a fool's decisions, and again, that takes getting wisdom first. Wisdom tells you not just how to proceed (to move or go forward) in the matter but how to precede (or go before).

Wisdom will *reverse a foolish decision!* Wisdom which provides you understanding will again reverse the consequences of a fool's decision!

Abigail's whole household was in danger because of her husband's unwise decision to not provide the king (who was David) at that time with what he requested of him. Listen to what King David said in his anger regarding this matter. "May God deal with David, be it ever so severely, if by morning I leave alive one male of all who belong to him!" (1 Samuel 25:22, NIV)

Nabel's foolish decision was going to bring a type of judgment upon all the men in their home! However, the wisdom of a woman halted all of this, thank God! Let's return to the scriptures to see what she did.

> When Abigail saw David, she quickly got off her donkey and bowed down before David with her face to the ground. She fell at his feet and said: "Pardon your servant, my lord, and let me speak to you; hear what your servant has to say. Please pay no attention, my lord, to that wicked man Nabal. He is just like his name—his name means Fool, and folly goes with him. And as for me, your servant, I did not see the men my lord sent. And now, my lord, as surely as the Lord your God lives and as you live, since the Lord has kept you from bloodshed and from avenging yourself with your own hands, may your enemies and all who are intent on harming my lord be like Nabal. And let this gift, which your servant has brought to my lord, be given to the men who follow you." "Please forgive your servant's presumption. The Lord your God will certainly make a lasting dynasty for my lord, because you fight the Lord's battles, and no wrongdoing will be found in you as long as you live. Even though someone is pursuing you to take your life, the life of my lord will be bound securely in the bundle of the living by the Lord your God, but the lives of your enemies he will hurl away as from the pocket of a sling. When the Lord has fulfilled for my lord every good thing he promised concerning him and has appointed him ruler over Israel, my lord will not have on his conscience the staggering burden of

needless bloodshed or of having avenged himself. And when the Lord your God has brought my lord success, remember your servant." David said to Abigail, "Praise be to the Lord, the God of Israel, who has sent you today to meet me. May you be blessed for your good judgment and for keeping me from bloodshed this day and from avenging myself with my own hands. Otherwise, as surely as the Lord, the God of Israel, lives, who has kept me from harming you, if you had not come quickly to meet me, not one male belonging to Nabal would have been left alive by daybreak." Then David accepted from her hand what she had brought him and said, "Go home in peace. I have heard your words and granted your request." (1 Samuel 25:23-35, NIV)

As you can see, Abigail, THE WISE WOMAN, realized that she needed to intercede when foolishness was at work because there are unwelcoming detrimental consequences to foolishness. We see Abigail immediately going into worship, we hear her speaking to the king with reverence, and we see her repentance on behalf of her husband's unwise decision to dishonor the king's request for food. We can say the wisdom of Abigail saved and preserved her household from the wrath of the king. Woman, likewise, will wisdom save your house too if you seek it *first*!

Lastly, let's recall again the proverb that says, "Every wise woman buildeth her house: but the foolish plucketh it down with her hands" (Proverbs 14:1).

Woman, even if you are married to a Nabal (a fool), wisdom can still be in your house if you, the Wise Woman, abide there! Your divine wisdom will save your household (and those in it) from the judgment of God, even if "foolishness" goes on in the house, or if a *fool resides in the house*. God does promise in His word *to save* you, woman, and *your house*. (See Acts 11:14.)

You just be sure, WOMAN, that SHE WISDOM is in the house!

CHAPTER 8

The Appointed Woman

And I came this day unto the well, and said, O Lord God of
my master Abraham, if now thou do prosper my way which
I go: Behold, I stand by the well of water; and it shall come
to pass, that when the virgin cometh forth to draw water,
and I say to her, Give me, I pray thee, a little water of thy
pitcher to drink; And she say to me, Both drink thou, and
I will also draw for thy camels: let the same be the woman
whom the Lord hath appointed out for my master's son.
—Genesis 24:42–44

As you may be noticing by now, I am beginning each chapter
with a Bible verse to show you, The Reader, that each composite of
The Woman (good or bad, godly or ungodly) that I am addressing
is *in the book* (or the Word of God). Therefore, even if The Woman
is bad or ungodly in kind, there is something that we can learn
from her that will lend to lessons in womanhood. So let's continue
looking at the various composites of THE WOMAN (in scripture)
by reviewing this Appointed Woman by the name of Rebekah.
Rebekah was the Appointed Woman that Abraham's servant prayed
for and met at the well. She was the woman appointed by God to
be Isaac's wife.

What does it mean to be *appointed*? Dictionary.com defines the word *appoint* as this:

- To name or assign by position
- To determine by authority or agreement
- To provide with what is necessary; equip

Therefore, we can say by this definition that the Appointed Woman has been named or (assigned) by position, she has been determined by some authority, and she has been equipped to provide that which is necessary! Wow, this sounds like a very POWERFUL WOMAN! I pray you are her in kind because this is not "every woman." *Real talk!* If this WOMAN is *you*, then congratulations! You should be humbled by your "positional placement," yet you should also be assured and confident that some authority backs your placement, for there is nothing like having the confidence to do what you do and be who you were sanctioned or positioned to be or become, knowing full well that *you possess the goods* for the assignment at hand. If an appointed woman is in a man's life like his wife or helpmeet, you are in a wonderful place of influence (not manipulation), and you must know that you, woman, *cannot be easily moved!* You should never forget that, especially if the authority that placed you there is GOD. So don't even try to move yourself, woman, for you have been equipped by the authority that put you there. Stay put and aim to do your assignment with grace.

Now let's go deeper.

That word *appointed* in our chapter opening scripture is *yakach* in Hebrew, and it simply means *to be right or correct*. Therefore, if you are the Appointed Woman, it means that you have been deemed or determined (even pre-determined) to be "the right one, baby," as the commercial says. You are the right or correct woman for the task, the work, or the job. Rebekah was equipped to draw water from the well for Abraham's servant and his camels. I always say I am a twenty-first century Rebekah because I can likewise draw "living water." Rebekah didn't complain about the labor involved. She obviously had the right muscles and enough energy to keep drawing water as needed.

Keep in mind, the servant said whichever woman could perform this task was an "appointed woman" by the Lord, and this woman was the woman to be Isaac's wife. Good job, Rebekah! God sanctioned your appointment. That's good news to the Appointed Woman, for you are not where you are by chance or accident. You have been divinely positioned and equipped for the task or job.

I am an Appointed Woman to do apostolic work, for it was predetermined by God that I would be a woman who is an Apostle! Please know, woman, there is an assurance that breeds confidence in your appointment. Your appointment, woman, lets you know you are right, correct, and equipped for the job, task, role, or the position in which you are being or have been appointed to.

Lastly, keep in mind; when you have an appointment, say, at the doctor, they are waiting for you, they are expecting you, and they are prepared to receive you, so, Woman, never take your appointment for granted, for it is such a blessing to be the Appointed Woman. Know this; some places you go require "an appointment" to be there. You cannot just show up! Selah (pause and think on this).

CHAPTER 9

The Blessed and Highly Favored Woman

And the angel came in unto her, and said, Hail, thou that art highly
favoured, the Lord is with thee: blessed art thou among women.
—Luke 1:28

I truly believe I am a blessed and highly favored woman. However,
my state of blessedness has nothing to do with my accumulations of
tangibles or natural endowments, although I am not in want either of
many things. Many people look at stuff and call themselves or others
"blessed" if they have a lot of "things" when this is in error! We cannot deduce the "blessings of God" to *stuff and things*!

Mary was a young virgin who was engaged to a man named
Joseph, and the angel Gabriel came and announced to her *first* that
she was highly favored and blessed among women. The word *blessed*
here means "to speak well of," and to be *highly favored* means "to be
graced or to endue with special honor or quality." Having stuff or
tangible things in great numbers doesn't make you blessed or favored,
for that matter. The blessing and *favor* takes its roots from Divinity
or God or the "God person," we can say. When you think of being
a "blessed and highly favored woman," isn't this an awesome woman
to be? One who is spoken well of and a woman who is graced and
endowed with a special honor or quality.

Well, when the angel Gabriel (who is a messenger angel) saluted
Mary, he said, "Hail thou that are…" That word *hail* is *chairo* in

Greek, and it is a greeting that means "to be cheerful and calmly happy"! It also means to "be well" and glad!

In other words, the angel Gabriel was sent to first announce to Mary her kingdom identity. Gabriel was saying to Mary, "Be cheerful or well, Mary, because you are graced, and you are well spoken of among women!"

Woman, if that is you, I salute you, too, with one word—*hail*! Well before Mary was told that she would be impregnated with Jesus she was told first of her own awesomeness and favor with God. Woman do know that God greatly uses those He favors. Favored ones are honored with great assignments. Just think how awesome it must have been to have been favored and blessed among all the women to be the mother of the Messiah, the Savior of the world! I must say that was quite a blessing to have been bestowed upon Mary. This young virgin woman got to be impregnated by the Holy Ghost, carry Christ (the word,) and then birth Christ (the word) out. What a blessing! Yet favored people are not void of troubles or woes. Mary's future husband wanted to privately put her away, but God intervened on her behalf by sending an angel to speak to Joseph to clarify to him Mary's assignment in the earth, and that, in essence, what she was carrying was a God thing. So if you are a favored and blessed woman, do know that God will always speak up for you. You don't have to ever defend the favor that's on your life. Be assured that the Lord will do it for you.

CHAPTER 10

The Leading Woman

And Deborah, a prophetess, the wife of
Lapidoth, she judged Israel at that time.

—Judges 4:4

We are in a time and dispensation where you will see Leading Women everywhere. Women leading in corporate America to women leading in major organizations, even women leading in the White House. In the year of 2017, we saw a woman run for president of these United States, and she had the potential, experience, even the qualifications to lead this country. Women are even leading local churches and church affiliations like parachurches and ministries of all kind. Therefore, I want to inform you that this will be a "lengthy" chapter, for I have much to cover that pertains to the Leading Woman, who is in great number in this day, with even more rising up to lead in accordance with their call.

I will start out by saying that women who lead are not exempt from the order of God where men were chosen for "headship" (and not just leadership), for the Bible does say this in 1 Corinthians 11:3. "But I would have you know that the head of every man is Christ, and the head of the woman is the man, and the head of Christ is God."

Think about this: Christ, the man and God, is a "head" above the rest!

Now there is a distinct difference between "headship," which is for the man to provide (not the woman), and "leadership," which both genders are capable of providing. Let's examine this more closely:

Headship and leadership can seem so similar, which is why when a woman is the Leading Woman, she can be viewed as attempting to "usurp" some "headship" in her life. However, this usually is not the case. Many women are leading ladies because God has graced and called them to lead, like Deborah, which we will discuss a little later in this chapter.

Leadership is simply "influence" to lead people, a corporation, organization, entity, etc. When you are a leader or a Leading Woman, you can (direct or guide) a person, a people, or an entity to its proper destination.

Headship, on the other hand, is *positioning*. The man has "upward" positional authority and not just "forward" or "frontal" positional influence, and *this is the order of God that we cannot change*, just as we cannot change the order of God as it relates to Jesus being *the great head* of the church. Allow me to give you a picture of what "headship" looks like to me, as I see an example of it in the scriptures concerning Saul, who was not only a newly appointed and anointed king (or leader) but also "head" of the people. Try to imagine headship in this scripture in 1 Samuel 10:23. "And they ran and fetched him thence: and when he stood among the people, he was higher than any of the people from his shoulders and upward."

So we as women must understand that "headship," which we all need, is not just a frontal or forward position of leadership, but it is, instead, a divine higher "upward" position of authority which God has designated for a man to abide in (not a woman). Therefore, I say to you, woman, you can most definitely be in leadership or be the Leading Woman, but you cannot be a "head," certainly for that is not by God's design for "any woman," no matter the kind to be in. I pray this enlightens you and causes you to have a greater respect for "the man" who heads you, and if you are the married woman, do know your head is your husband and not your pastor.

Now let's go even deeper, as it relates to the man being *the head* of the woman. *Head* (as mentioned in 1 Corinthians 11:3) is *kephale* in the Greek, and it is taken from the primary word *kapto* (meaning in the sense of seizing) with *the head* as being the part most readily taken hold of, literally or figuratively. So when we look at headship, we can now understand why God positioned *the man* to "head" the woman, just as He positioned Jesus in a position that allows Him to "head" the church (a she or a bride). Headship is for protection purposes (first). Listen to Genesis 3:15: "And I will put enmity between thee and the woman, and between thy seed and her seed; it shall bruise thy head, and thou shalt bruise his heel." God spoke this to the serpent, letting him know that Jesus's headship would bruise by seizing his head, and all Satan could do is bruise His heel, for truly, Satan is under His feet. I pray you can see the importance of having headship, woman. Headship is "upward" positional authority that is given to us as women and the church or the bride of Christ. Hear this scripture in Ephesians 1:19–21:

> And what is the exceeding greatness of his power to us-ward who believe, according to the working of his mighty power, Which he wrought in Christ, when he raised him from the dead, and set him at his own right hand in the heavenly places, Far above all principality, and power, and might, and dominion, and every name that is named, not only in this world, but also in that which is to come.

Just look at what God did in terms of Jesus's headship:

- He (God) raised him (from the dead)!
- He (God) set him!
- He (God) positioned him "far above all"!

Woman please know that "headship" and all that it entails is a God thing! It is something that is ordained by God, and it should not be negated or altered in any way. It is not a "position of authority" for the woman, but "headship" has been ordained for "the man," Jesus, and God Himself!

Therefore, prayerfully, WOMAN, you can now better understand that headship is vitally necessary to you as a woman and should not be "avoided" because it is for "protective purposes" for you, and headship personifies the order of God. Now I will agree that there may be men who use headship to lord over a woman or to dominate a woman, and these reasons are not keeping with God's purpose of headship. I know also that many women avoid the headship of their husbands because they do not see them as a "good leader," for he lacks leadership skills, say, in the home. Truly, that might be the case; however, God does not "cut off" the head of a man because he is not a good leader. He instead holds that man accountable, and he leaves him in his position of authority because, again, remember, headship is not just "leadership," it's a *protective position* of authority ordained by God to protect *you,* the woman. So you, woman, must allow Christ Jesus to "head him." Keep in mind, woman, that man could be there (in position) for "protective reasons" solely, meaning only simply to *cover you.* For if there is a demonic seizure, the enemy is coming for "his head" (first), not yours, if you are covered. So you must pray fervently for your head.

Note: When the officiating minister asks at the wedding cere-mony, "Who gives this woman to be married to this man," he's ask-ing this question usually to the father of the bride or "the man" that walked her down the aisle. This question prompts "the father of the bride" or "the man" to say, "I do," and this signals that there is about to be a *change of headship,* or we can say, a "transference of headship" for this woman, which is why it is customary for a man to ask the woman's father if he can marry his daughter *before* he proposes to her. A father is the man who covers (or heads) the daughter, not the mother. The father in her life provides "headship" for her, not her mother. So when the daughter "weds," she now becomes the woman who will no longer be covered (or headed) by her father but by her husband instead. Therefore, a woman must be "given away" by the man who had the responsibility of covering her as her head. Again, this is a divine responsibility of a man (not a woman); which is why I am not in favor of "mothers" walking their daughters down the aisle, for it says, I am a woman with no headship or no covering, and this is not in alignment with God's order! My last point on headship is this: Headship is ordained by God for ALL WOMEN, leading women or not. Headship is a spiritual covering for the woman, and if you are a single woman headed down the aisle to be married to a man, the exchange of "headship" will occur at the altar, and your father will give you away to another man to *head you*. Please know you were never meant to be a "headless woman" (i.e. a woman void of protection or a covering).

Now let's look at this Leading Woman, Deborah, as we conclude this chapter. For reason of God's own choosing, God decided to use a woman, who was a wife and a prophetess, to judge the children of Israel after the death of Ehud (a man judge), and while they were sold into captivity into the hand of Jabin, the king of Canaan, according to Judges chapter four, never in the history of Israel did God use a woman in this capacity. However, the time came where he decided to select a woman to not only "judge" but to also enter "willingly" into a battle with Barak, the commander of the army, at his request. Listen to what Barak (this Leading Man) said to this Leading Woman in Judges 4:8: "And Barak said unto her, If thou wilt go with me, then I will go: but if thou wilt not go with me, then I will not go."

The Bible is silent on this; however, for some reason, Barak refused to go into battle without this Leading Woman named Deborah. Could it be because she was a prophetess and Barak knew that her prophetic ministry would be directional to him and his team? Again, the Bible is silent on this; all we know is that Barak was not going after Israel's enemy, Sisera, without this Leading Woman accompanying him, and Deborah did prophesy the journey they were embarking upon.

However, here's what I would like to bring out about this Leading Woman and what I think is worth mentioning to all the "potential leaders" who are women. *If you are going to be a leading woman, you must arise* to the occasion and the opportunity. This is what I saw Deborah had to do to take her leadership of being a judge to the next level of leadership, and that is, she had to arise to the occasion and the opportunity. Listen to Deborah's reply to Barak's "call to duty" to her: "And she said, I will surely go with thee: notwithstanding the journey that thou takest shall not be for thine honour; for the Lord shall sell Sisera into the hand of a woman. And Deborah arose, and went with Barak to Kedesh."

If you are going to be a Leading Woman, then you are going to have to answer your call and not miss your appointment either. THEN YOU MUST ARISE TO THE OCASSION OR THE OPPORTUNITY TO LEAD. You can't remain "complacent or comfortable" per say if you're going to be a Leading Woman, YOU MUST ARISE!

Deborah was a wife, a prophetess, a judge, but then she arose as something else as a Leading Woman, and guess what it was? *A mother to a nation!* By going after the enemy who was oppressing the children of Israel with the Leading Man (Barak), Deborah arose as a mother to the children of Israel, and the scriptures shows us this by way of a song that Deborah came back singing in victory in Judges 5:7, which says, "The inhabitants of the villages ceased, they ceased in Israel, until that I Deborah arose, that I arose a mother in Israel."

Therefore, Deborah moved from a "place of comfort," that being from under the palm tree, and she arose to the presented occasion by Barak. Deborah grabbed hold of the opportunity to be *a next level* Leading Woman right there beside a Leading Man; both operating in their sphere of gifting and authority to take down the enemies of the Lord, allowing the children to benefit from their victory together. This is a beautiful depiction of team leadership and kingdom partnership that the Bible presents to us as we look at the joint efforts of two leaders by the name of Barak and Deborah. Therefore, it is always my hope that Leading Men and Leading Women will come together in leadership to ignite more victories in God, for surely our children need more victories in their lives too. Just think what would happen if mothers and fathers teamed up to go after the enemies that are oppressing our children. Surely, *greater victories* would manifest. I strongly support and am in favor of team efforts led by a man and woman, naturally and spiritually.

CHAPTER 11

The Saved Woman

And he said to the woman, Thy faith hath saved thee; go in peace.
—Luke 7:50

I am so glad this woman here in Luke chapter 7 was left name-less. Although if you study the Bible closely, you will later discover in the book of John that this woman who Jesus saved by forgiving her of her sins (which we will talk more about in the next chapter) was Mary of Bethany, the sister of Martha and Lazarus, all of whom became very good friends of Jesus. This assures me that, regardless of our past and our past lifestyles, we, as women, can be forgiven by the Lord and partake also in this wonderful gift of salvation. Then through a personal relationship, we, too, like Mary of Bethany, can progress in becoming a "friend of God" through Christ Jesus. The Saved Woman, who is a "forgiven woman," can progress into friend-ship with Christ Jesus if she moves into establishing an intimate and personal relationship with Him.

One thing I never wanted as a Saved Woman was a "one-time" experience or encounter with Jesus, I wanted to know more about the one who saved me. To be "saved" (SOZO) in the Greek means to be delivered and protected. When Jesus told that woman that her faith "hath saved" her, and that she could now go in peace (which was something she did not have prior); it meant that she had been healed and preserved. This woman could now "do well" and had been made whole. Well, anyone that can do that for me warrants a pursuit of a relationship with, and that's exactly what this now-Saved Woman named Mary of Bethany did. She later invited Jesus to her house, and in the book of John, we now see this Saved Woman positioned again at the feet of Jesus but, this time, feasting on the word of God.

This Biblical Saved Woman is to be modeled by other saved women. Every Saved Woman should pursue an intimate personal relationship with Christ, and again, not just have a one-time encounter with Jesus. Every Saved Woman should invite Jesus into their house (i.e. their inner being) and sup with Him. Every Saved Woman should be experiencing wholeness and healing, all while doing well in life. The Saved Woman should be experiencing the preservation and peace that a life in Christ avails her. Another thing that Jesus pointed out to the men in the room besides the "anointing of the oil," which I will talk about in the next chapter, was that this woman loved much. Listen to what Jesus said to the men in the room about this. "Wherefore, I say unto thee, Her sins, which are many, are forgiven, *for she loved much*: but to whom little is forgiven, the same loveth little" (Luke 7:47; italics added).

This woman's faith caused her to enter the room where Jesus was with a bunch of men who she probably knew would condemn her; however, her expressed love for Jesus (through her worship of Him) caused her "many sins" to be forgiven. Surely, you, likewise, as the Saved Woman, can also expressively love the Lord as well. Just think on John 3:16 and remember that God loved you first. Always remember, Saved Woman, you should be a friend of Jesus and a woman who is faith-filled, full of love for the Lord, and always endeavoring to walk in peace thereof.

CHAPTER 12

The Sinner Woman

And, behold a woman in the city, which was a sinner,
when she knew that Jesus sat at meat in the Pharisee's
house, brought an alabaster box of ointment,
—Luke 7:37

As we continue to look at this same woman which I discussed in the previous chapter who I disclosed as being Mary of Bethany, I chose to introduce her first as a saved woman and then look back at her as being the same Sinner Woman who knew where Jesus was, whose house he was in, and even what He was doing in the house. Don't you ever think that sinners don't watch Christians. They are watching who you are with, whose house you go to, and what you are doing when you are there even. The above passage of scripture says: "When she knew that Jesus sat at meat in the Pharisee's house," that's when she entered that house (with her oil) and stood at the feet of Jesus behind Him, weeping, began to wash His feet with her tears, and did wipe them with the hair of her head. This Sinner Woman kissed the feet of Jesus and anointed them with the ointment that she brought with her. I truly believe that it is what the Sinner Woman had previously seen or recognized about Jesus that ignited her with the faith she needed to enter that house. Again the Scripture says when she knew that Jesus sat at meat. If I may phantom in my mind, perhaps the woman had been waiting for Jesus to make His way to that house before she ventured in. Based on the way the Pharisee spoke of the Sinner Woman, she was obviously known in that city for her sin nature, yet the Pharisee did not think Jesus (the Prophet) knew or recognized who she was. I truly believe Jesus looked "beyond" her many sins and saw her need, which was forgiveness. The old saints would say it like this: "He looked beyond my faults and he saw my needs." The Bible tells us in 1 Samuel 16:7 that the Lord does not see the way man sees, for man looks on the outward appearance, but the Lord looks on the heart. So apparently, Jesus first looked at this woman and revealed a heart filled with faith, then He saw how she used her oil. She poured it out on Him. While everybody was looking and seeing the sin in this woman's life, Jesus saw that her faith, her love for Him which was exhibited through her worship, was enough to forgive The Sinner Woman.

So if you are a Sinner Woman reading this book, if you have a grain of a mustard seed of faith in your heart, I pray, by reading this book, that your faith will be stirred to look up, see, and recognize Jesus through God's goodness and mercy that's been following you all the days of your life. I pray that you, the Sinner Woman, allows Jesus to cause you (by faith) to be the Saved Woman, which I talked about in the previous chapter, for this is the same woman. You too can move from being a Sinner Woman to the Saved Woman by grace if you would just repent and accept Jesus as your own personal Savior. If you are ready, woman, to be forgiven of your sins, recite this prayer below with me.

Heavenly Father,

I come to you in prayer asking for forgiveness of my sins. I confess with my mouth and I believe with my heart that Jesus is your only begotten Son, who died not just for the sins of the world but mine also. Lord, I accept Jesus (your Son) as my Savior, the one who shed his blood for my sins. I accept that I have been bought with a price, and that it was His blood that redeemed me from the penalty of my sins.

Father, I believe with my whole heart that Jesus died on the cross and rose from the dead. I ask right now, Father, that your Son Jesus come into my heart and my life and be my personal Lord and Savior.

Father, I repent for my sins and ask, dear Father, that you cleanse me and wash me clean as snow. I thank you right now, Father, and I know and believe that you do hear The Sinner's Prayer of Repentance and you do, Father, give sinners an opportunity to worship you when they come to Jesus. I thank you, Father God. It's in Jesus's name I pray. Amen.

Woman, if you have prayed this prayer, then you are saved now and I, along with the angels, are now rejoicing over the saving of your soul. I will be praying for you that you will now seek out a pastor and a church home where you can be fed and discipled in the faith as you connect in fellowship with other believers. If you just got saved, *do not forsake* assembling with other believers, and now would be a good time to go buy a Bible or download a Bible app on your phone "for free." I encourage you, woman, to start reading the gospel according to John first, for it will enlighten you about the light of Christ. *Keep your Bible handy* for it's loaded with the Word of God which you will need to grow and learn the ways God, along with His plan for your life. Do know, woman, God's promises for your life have already been predetermined; however, you need to discover it, and His word will help you do just that i.e. discover His will for your life. You can rest assured, woman, that God's got plans *for you,* and now that you are saved, you can enter thou into His plans and purposes too. You are ready to go forward, for Jesus has saved, rescued, and redeemed you as the now-Saved Woman who used to be the Sinner Woman. Truly, this is a great place to give the Lord praise, for now your sins, woman, are now *covered* and *under the blood!* So, *go* and sin *no more,* for this chapter was written just for you.

CHAPTER 13

The Worshipping Woman

And a certain woman named Lydia, a seller of purple,
of the city of Thyatira, which worshiped God, heard
us: whose heart the Lord opened, that she attended
unto the things which were spoken of Paul

—Acts 16:14

I want to start this chapter out by saying this: The woman who worships has an open heart to God and the things of God. The woman who worships can always be found attending to the things of the Lord, for worship will always take you right into *the holy place* where God is the focus. Another thing; the woman who worships "hears from God" for herself, for God always reveals things in worship.

It takes having reverence and adoration for something or someone (other than yourself) to worship. It takes placing something or someone "higher than yourself" to worship them. Worship will always take the focus off you, and worship requires a "selfless" type of adoration for something or another. Yes, you can praise God yet not be a worshipper, because often, when people praise God, they are praising or thanking God for what He did for them. However, worship has nothing to do with you! It's all about the one you are releasing adoration for, and prayerfully, you are worshipping THE LORD, THE MOST HIGH GOD ALMIGHTY, ELOHIM, THE CREATOR OF ALL!

The Scripture tells us in John 4:23 that the Father seeks a true worshipper that can worship him in spirit and in truth. You cannot be a carnal worshipper, for you would be too "hostile" towards the things of God to worship him. You can't worship God being sensual either, because you're worshipping a God that you can't physically touch, see, smell, or even hear with an "audible voice," for we are no longer in that dispensation where God speaks in an audible voice. Instead, you must be *spiritual* if you are going to worship the Father in "spirit and truth."

The Worshipping Woman is a woman who desires the Father (Abba) in personhood and not just the Father's goods, and the Father knows if you are a woman that wants Him or if you are simply seeking his goods. Know this, Father God is not likened unto "a sugar daddy," and He knows if you are seeking "His Face" or if you just want what's in "His Hand." Trust me, He knows the difference and He is a good, enlightened Father who knows how to give "good gifts" to His children.

If we look at Lydia, the named woman in our chapter's opening scripture, more than likely, her merchant business (as being a seller of purple) brought her great riches. Lydia was not worshipping God for stuff or things. However, I can assure you that I have never spent time in "worship" and not come away with something of a deposit into my spirit being. Yet my goal for worship with the Father was simply to "extol" Him. It was to tell Him how important He is to me. Worship is all about the awesomeness of your Heavenly Father; however, let's zoom back into the scriptures and look at this Worshipping Woman by the name of Lydia.

The Bible calls her a "certain woman." When I read the Bible, I have learned, and was even taught, to pay attention to "words," for often, the Holy Spirit will show you something that is hidden in the *Logos* (i.e. the written Word of God), that revelation will uncover. That word *certain* means "of a kind," so we can say Lydia was of a particular "kind of woman." This highlights the essence of why I believe God inspired me to write this book; so that you, the woman reading this book, could discover the "kind" of woman you are. Therefore, with each chapter, I have sought to elaborate on the "makeup" (and

I don't mean MAC or L'Oréal) of the highlighted woman, which shows or identifies "the composite" of this kind of woman, along with her "disparate" or her distinction in kind because differences do vary in kind. I must stop here and tell you I have known for a long time (since childhood) that I was "different in kind." As a matter of fact, my mother always (on a regular basis) told me that *I was different* in kind. When I would ask her why, she did not allow me to do or engage in what other girls were doing; her reply was always this: "Because you are different." I did not see myself like the other girls in my neighborhood, for the composite of Sharon as a maturing young lady was showing me as being different in kind. I can even recall others saying these words to me: "You're different." Although I did not fully understand my distinction back then or the purpose for the distinction, today I do. I now know that "my distinction" in kind was synonymous with my purpose in kind as a woman, for my purpose is to be *the standard of holiness* for women. The composite of who I am was not meant to be common; however, it was meant to be "a rule or a model" for other women. *This was God's design* of Sharon, for it was not mine, yet it is for me to accept, and I do. I know my kind and can recognize my kind quite readily. What we all share as women universally is that we are *all female*; however, our composite as a woman is distinct in kind. So the statement, "You women are *all alike*," is a lie that came from Hell or from some originator who did not make woman in kind.

Again, back to this "certain" woman named Lydia who worshipped God. Her very name means "A Christian Woman;" therefore, we should all agree that a Christian Woman should be of the kind of woman who worships; however, we do have Christian women who are not a Lydia who I will call women of the kind who worship! If you are going to call yourself a Christian Woman, please be of "the kind" that worships God. Otherwise, you just might be viewed as Christian but of some other kind, for "saints" do come as all kinds, according to Ephesians 3:18.

There are many examples of worshipping women in the gospels who fell to their knees and worshipped the Lord. The word *worship* is an Old and a New Testament word, and that word superseded the word *Christian* or the Christian faith. Even before the word *Christian* was used, worship was a part of heaven and the kingdom of God. Therefore, the Worshipping Woman is not just a Christian woman by faith or belief, she is a woman who pays "homage" to her Lord. The Worshipping Woman is a woman who "bows herself," one who will "fall down" to do or make "obeisance" (or reverence) to her God. This is of the kind that Lydia was. This is the kind of woman that had the power to *constrain* the man of God, Apostle Paul. Listen to what she said to the man of God after he baptized her and her house-hold. "If ye have judged me to be faithful to the Lord, come into my house, and abide there. And she constrained us" (Acts 16:15).

There are three things I want to leave you with in this chapter about the Worshipping Woman.

The Worshipping Woman is a safe woman for men of God to be around and even do ministry with, for this woman is about the business of God. She has no mixed agendas. Notice this woman, unlike the Strange Woman, which we discussed earlier in this book, has no intentions which are evil as it relates to the man coming into her house. Therefore, the man of God had no reservations about abiding there!

The Worshipping Woman has "compelling" power! She does not need to manipulate, use flattery or any other "ungodly" practices to cause someone to abide. The scripture says that Lydia (the wor-shipping woman) in kind constrained them. She "entreated" them, and they simply abode in her house, void of any funny business or any inordinance. However, here is the last thing I will say about the Worshipping Woman.

Lydia said to the man of God, "If you judge me to be faith-ful to the Lord… Come into my house"! I absolutely love what the Word of God is showing us about this woman in kind. Lydia, the worshipping woman was saying, "You be the judge man of God and only if you judge me as *faithful to the Lord* should you come into my house," otherwise, keep it moving! Again, this is so powerful, Woman, because it shows us who the Worshipping Woman's alle-giance is to (i.e. her God), the Lord. This shows us her agenda as well, and it is centered on the Lord. The Worshipping Woman is so focused on the Lord that she does not "shun" being judged to be pure, holy, and authentically godly in her motives and her intentions.

Therefore, if you are of this kind of woman, I simply say *bravo*, heaven applauds you, Woman; for truly you can "rightly "represent the Kingdom of God as a woman of faith and as a Christian woman who worships the true and Living God.

CHAPTER 14

The Married Woman

But she that is married careth for the things of the
world, how she may please her husband.

—Corinthian 7:34b

Whenever you see the word *but* in a sentence, it cancels out what was previously said for the continuance of the sentence. *But* is like an exception word for whatever comes after it. All applies in the sentence until you see the word *but*, for that word announces a new thought. This is the case with the above scripture, which prior to the *but*, Paul was addressing the "unmarried woman," with which she will be addressed in the next chapter. Therefore, I will not address what was said "before" the "but" in this chapter. Instead, I will address what the writer said "after" the "but" concerning the Married Woman, for we see her cares are different than the unmarried woman.

Paul said the Married Woman cares for the things of the world, for she must figure out how she may please "not the Lord" but her husband, for this is her responsibility. You see, "married folk" have cares, and this was not a care that Apostle Paul wanted for himself. I truly believe that marriage takes "maturity" because you have "spousal responsibilities" as marrieds. Marriage is not something that should be entered lightly but with much prayer and counsel should a man and woman marry.

Now it is in this chapter that I will make some quotes and references from my book called *Help for the Help Meet*, which I highly recommend you read if you are the Married Woman, for it will greatly help you better understand your role as a man's *helpmeet*. In this book, I wrote about this in chapter four, which I entitled "You Are His Care." Allow me to share more of what I wrote. When you are a man's helpmeet, you now have the responsibility of "caring" for your husband. The care of your husband is not a care that you can cast to God, because that man's care is now in your hands, not God's. This means you must seek ways to please him. This type of care lies within your responsibility as his helpmeet. This is not his mother's job or any other woman's job, but it's *yours* as his helpmeet.

When you are the Married Woman, you cannot be so busy with the cares of other things that you don't seek to care for your husband. First Corinthians 7 lets us know that the Married Woman is busy with the "things of the world," trying to please her husband. In my above referenced book, I explain what this means, so allow me to share it with you.

In the Greek translation, the world is *kosmos*, and it means orderly arrangement i.e. decoration. Think about it the way God created the world; he did it in an "orderly arrangement," and he decorated it accordingly. Now that word, *kosmos* (Strong's Concordance Number G2889), takes its root word from the Greek word, *komizo* (Strong's Concordance Number G2865), which means "to tend" or "take care of properly." It also means "to provide for" or "to carry off." This means that as a wife or the Married Woman, you must seek ways to tend to or take care of your husband in a natural way. If we put these two Greek words together to define "things of the world," then we can say that the Married Woman cares or tends to her husband when she seeks ways to "adorn or decorate" herself (or his surroundings) in a way that pleases his natural man! Which means if you are the Married Woman, you must take off the prayer shawl and perhaps adorn yourself with something that is "naturally" pleasing to him, like some lingerie or stilettos. Woman of God, I'm glad you have a prayer life and can pray for your husband's spirit man, but you also have a responsibility as the Married Woman, to appeal and appease or please *his natural man*. Therefore, do know, as the Married Woman, you are permitted to put your Bible down and cook your husband a good meal or go out with him or allow him to "see" your natural goods as you seek to "minister to his natural man" (as unto the Lord). Therefore, sex is meant for marrieds because it is so pleasing (or should be) for both the husband and the wife, naturally speaking. Never feel guilty as a married woman, for coming away from the "things of God" to attend to the "things of the world" to please your husband, God permits it. Do know this, Married Woman, you can *rock* your husband's world since you are in it, and God permits you as the Married Woman to do just that. As a matter of truth, He wants you to do this the same way He wants the Unmarried woman to tend to the things of the Lord. So don't let your spirituality get in the way of you simply being a natural woman to your husband.

CHAPTER 15

The Unmarried Woman

> There is a difference also between a wife and a virgin.
> The unmarried woman careth for the things of the Lord,
> that she may be holy both in body and in spirit.
> —Corinthian 7:34

There is so much that's in the Word of God to keep and preserve us, yet often, we "miss the mark" because we don't adhere to His word. However, thank God for Jesus, who redeems us from sin and allows us a new beginning in Him. I started this chapter out this way to remove "condemnation" and guilt away from the Unmarried Woman who is *not* a virgin. If you notice, the above scripture starts out by saying *there is a difference* between a wife (or a married woman) and a virgin. What's the difference, you may ask? Answer: The Unmarried Woman is not supposed to have "man cares," as she is only supposed to care for the things of the Lord, for this keeps her holy in her body and in her spirit. When the Unmarried Woman starts "tending to" the cares of a man and how to please him (which, as I mentioned in the previous chapter, is the responsibility of a wife), which you are not if you are single, then she will more than likely have to compromise her "holiness" to please him. Please hear me, Unmarried Woman; pleasing a man is *not* your responsibility because you are not *his wife*. The Unmarried Woman should not have this care, but you should be focused and diligent in pleasing the Lord. You should be caring for or tending to the "things of the Lord," for this care contributes to your holiness in your body and your spirit. You should be "available" too, for the things of God. You should be in prayer often! You should be in Bible study! You should be "actively" working and serving in the house of the Lord, for it will keep you holy and away from the cares associated with a man. When a man finds you, he ought to find you, the unmarried woman in the Lord. In other words, if he is looking for you, he's got to come over to where the "things of the Lord" is to find you. He should not find you in the field looking for some man to give you a name. He just might give you a name, woman, but it won't be his last name. Selah (pause and think on that)!

Far too many unmarried women, or single women as we call them today, are so tied up and tangled up with men or a man that have no intention of marrying them. It's a complete waste of your time, woman. It's taking you away from the things of the Lord, and again you can count on your holiness being comprised in body or spirit. Okay, I can hear the Unmarried Woman saying, "Well, how can I get married if I don't date?" All right, let's address dating. First, "dating" is not in the Bible. It's not a biblical word. However, let's define the word *date*. A date is a "social appointment" or engagement arranged (beforehand) with another person. Now if you as an unmarried woman have a "date" that is an occurrence or an appointment or an engagement; fine, go on a date and come back to the "things of the Lord." However, usually that is not the case, if you are honest. A date leads to "dating," which now involves some kind of romantic involvement, which often no longer has anything to do with an occurrence or an appointment, and certainly "no engagement" is involved. If you go to that man's house, does that constitute as a date? If he comes to your house, is that now a date? No, it does not in its meaning by definition. What you are now involved in with this man is not a date. What you are calling "dating" is really an unmarried relationship with a potential spouse perhaps. If that is the case, then I call that "courting for marriage." However, let's call it what it really is because some of those relationships last a month, four months, nine months, one year, or ten years void of marriage. Usually by then, as an unmarried "saved" woman, you have long left focusing on caring for (or attending to) the things of the Lord, and that man has become your focus. Not to mention that, more than likely, again, your holiness in Him has been compromised or aborted all together so that you can "properly" please this man, which usually involves premarital sex, which is fornication. Again, please know that the only woman that is permitted to focus on pleasing a man is the Married Woman. You are probably saying now, "Then what should I do" as an Unmarried Woman. Simple, find contentment in being a woman who pleases the Lord, for you will be surprised what He might do for you if your focus is on Him. Trust the Lord as it relates to your desire for a mate, but don't go looking for a mate, seeing that is not your responsibility as the Unmarried Woman. Find happiness in your singleness. Truly, the Lord knows that, if you can be faithful in seeking to please Him, then He can trust that He can allow a faithful man of God to find you to be his wife and then seek to please him as your husband. Unmarried Woman, as it relates to caring for a man, you can *cast that care for now* because it is not yours.

Lastly, if you are indeed the Unmarried Woman in the faith, *do not* mirror the practices of the world as it relates to relationships, for it is full of lustful intents and motives. Replace the word *dating* with *fellowship*, for that is mentioned and approved in the Word of God among believers.

CHAPTER 16

The Barren Woman

He maketh the barren woman to keep house, and to
be a joyful mother of children. Praise ye the Lord.
—Psalm 113:9

Infertility, as many women deal with *today*, is not new, and it is just as frustrating and painful now as it was for the barren women in the Bible. The Bible clearly highlights the agony of women who were barren in those days. Allow me to give you the names of some "noted" barren women in the Bible, and notice how I present their barrenness (i.e. as women who eventually had a child or children) which should encourage you if you are this woman in kind.

- Isaac's mother (Sarah), who was married to Abraham, was barren.
- Jacob's mother (Rebekah), who was married to Isaac, was barren.
- Joseph's mother (Rachel), who was married to Jacob, was barren.
- Samson's mother, an "unnamed woman" who was married to Manoah, was barren.

- Samuel's mother (Hannah), who was married to Elkanah, was barren.
- Elizabeth, John the Baptist's mother, who was married to Zachariah the High priest, was barren.

Notice all these women were barren but eventually had children, which is why I chose to use the above scripture to open this chapter. It shows that "barrenness" is addressed by God Himself in the Bible, seeing that "children" are the heritage of the Lord and considered a fruitful reward. I think God is "merciful," and the Bible proves that he can also address the Barren Woman's condition. Therefore, it is in this chapter that I want to encourage the Barren Woman who is trying to have children that cannot thus far. I am hoping that this woman in kind will not lose hope, because I have heard of, and do know personally, several barren women who now have a child speak of their conception as nothing short of a miracle. I personally have prayed for the womb of the Barren Woman, beseeching God to open it up to conceive. I remember there was a woman on my job when I was in corporate America who could not have children. She had tried fertility specialists, only to lose the fertilized eggs after in vitro fertilization. After deciding not to continue with in vitro and just wait on God, years later, the Lord simply opened her womb and she conceived. She named the baby girl Grace. For many barren women, I think the wait with a "ticking clock" is what bothers the Barren Woman. Not to mention the constant inquiries from friends and family as to why you have no children yet, which can be a constant reminder of your barrenness and can be quite embarrassing as well. Like Hannah, being around other women with children or around women who "constantly" get pregnant makes being barren a hard pill to swallow. Then many women who deal with barrenness have to also deal with the "monthly" reminder of not being pregnant by having a menstrual cycle, which does not help either. I'm certain this is quite painful because the Barren Woman often keeps hope alive for years that, one day, she will conceive and be with child. As with these Biblical barren women, when they did conceive, it shows us the *power of God* at work in the womb of a woman. I say all the time the womb is a place of divinity. However, the womb of a woman is also a place for demonic attack, too, because many women suffer pain or complications with female problems, as the Old Mothers would call the infirmities of the womb. Again I have laid hands on the wombs of many women to be healed of their "womb infirmities." Fibroid tumors, cervical and uterine cancer, endometriosis, cysts, tubal pregnancies, not to mention the various vaginal infections that plague women are all "womb related" because even the vagina serves as a "passageway for birthing life." So I encourage women to lay hands on their own womb and pray while pleading the blood of Jesus over their wombs because, again, Satan knows that the womb is a place of divinity. To many barren women, it can feel like a curse, but I do not believe your womb is "cursed;" however, it may be "closed" to birthing for a season or time, yet God can open it by healing the Barren Woman's womb.

Note: There were about seven barren women in the Bible, six of them I named above. All but one of these barren women's wombs were healed, and they eventually birthed a child or children. However, there was Michal, David's first wife (Saul's daughter) who was barren, but God did not heal her womb; instead, she remained "barren" until the day of her death, so says 2 Samuel 6:23. To me, this was out of the norm for God, and I wanted to know why, so you must read up in the chapter of 2 Samuel 6 to find out why God didn't heal her of her barrenness. Allow me to share with you my discovery.

King David had allowed the Ark of the Covenant to go to and remain in the house of Obededom the Gittite when he got mad because God "smote" or killed Uzzah when he touched the Ark of the Covenant when it almost fell. However, when King David heard how blessed Obededom's house was because of the Ark of the Covenant being there (which was symbolic of the presence of God), he went and brought the Ark of the Covenant (or the presence of God) back into the city of David. He was so glad to get the Ark of the Covenant back in the city that David did an "undignified" praise in front of everybody. Well, his wife, Michal, saw her husband praising God like that, and she despised him dancing like that in front of his handmaidens. She felt he had shamed himself as a king. Listen how King

David responded and then take note as to what is mentioned afterwards regarding his wife Michal.

> David said to Michal, "It was before the Lord, who chose me rather than your father or anyone from his house when he appointed me ruler over the Lord's people Israel—I will celebrate before the Lord. I will become even more undignified than this, and I will be humiliated in my own eyes. But by these slave girls you spoke of, I will be held in honor." And Michal daughter of Saul had no children to the day of her death.

So here we can see that there seems to be some correlation between Michal being guilty of despising what God esteems (which in this instance is praise), and her barrenness. Sarah laughed when she was told she would conceive, yet that did not cause a lifetime of barrenness. She did eventually conceive in her nineties. My point is this; in most instances with the Barren Woman, God heals her womb thus enabling her to bear children or a child. Again, six out of seven Biblical barren women's wombs did God heal, causing fertility. The Barren Woman that did not get healed in the womb and the woman who remained barren until her death was the woman that despised *praise*. So I say to the Barren Woman, don't stop praising God, and don't stop loving what God loves, no matter how long it takes for you to conceive. To the Barren Woman, I say lastly; regardless of your barren condition, try to remember that six out of seven women God healed of barrenness. Perhaps if Michal had repented of her sin, she would have been in the number of healed barren women too, for truly, we know God to be a forgiving God. Hannah admitted to the priest in the temple that she was a sorrowful woman, and she poured out her anger and frustration right there where her cries and her repentance was heard by God. So you can express to God how you feel as a barren woman. You can ask for prayer regarding your barrenness, just don't stop praising God, woman! Finally, to the Barren Woman, I say stay hopeful, prayerful, and continue to expect to one day be "expecting," for God can heal your womb. His track record in the Bible proves that he cares for the Barren Woman. Again, I leave you with the opening chapter scripture as my way of encouraging you, the Barren Woman.

> He maketh the barren woman to keep house, and to be a joyful mother of children. Praise ye the Lord. (Psalm 113:9)

CHAPTER 17

The Free Woman

But he of the freewoman was by promise.

—Galatians 4:23b

The promises of God are not attached to bondage. You have got to get out of bondage if you're going to be free. Liberty or freedom is something that Jesus avails us as those who believe in Him. The Bible lets us know that whom the Son sets free is *free indeed*.

The scripture lets us know that Jesus was full of grace and truth. Freedom is rooted in *truth*. This means you can *never* be a free woman operating in lies, deception, or pretense. Therefore, you can't lie to yourself or about yourself and be the Free Woman. You can't be "delusional" and think you are free. You cannot be deceptive and free. Lies, delusions, and deceptions will keep you bound and in bondage, which is the opposite of being free or at liberty. Jesus Christ will *always* set at liberty a people, for He too knows that the promises of God are attached to the person who is free to serve Him. The goal of heaven is to get you free, woman, then the fulfillment of the promises of God for your life can now come to pass.

I remember I hosted a women's revival through my women's ministry, Sweet Rose of Sharon, and that year, my focus was on "the

Free Woman," for that was my theme. Allow me to share the introduction of my message. I said:

> If you are going to remain a free woman you cannot allow yourself to wander away from truth by delving into falsity and false teachings because if you do you will find yourself being entangled (again) with a yoke of bondage.

So since "freedom" is a good thing, if you are reading this chapter and you believe that you are the Free Woman in kind, then let me give you more insight of what this says about you in kind.

The essence of the Free Woman is that you have moved ahead and out of the shadow of your past. This is really a good place to praise God, for so many women can't seem to get past that shadow, for it follows them like a plague everywhere they go and into their relationships, even. However, the Free Woman has progressed in the direction of the *promise* of her future! If that's you, woman, I applaud you because you are an overcomer, and you are now free to pursue life without the shadow of failures, bad decisions, or mistakes. The Free Woman has embraced the pangs of her now, for she sees these pains as "growing pains," which are a part of the journey to her new territory where promise resides.

The Free Woman is a "destined woman," and she is purposely en route to her *promised land*. Again, woman, if this is *you*, I say bravo to you, because you are (as a free woman) *always* on your way. Truly, in Christ do you live, move, and have your being. The Free Woman is a "fellow yoke woman" with Christ, for you go where He goes. You go where the Spirit leads you.

You, the Free Woman, have overcome much, and even if you were led into the wilderness, you won't be found "crying there," and neither will you stay there, but you are the kind of woman who sees the wilderness as a destined route to your land of promise.

The Free Woman is free from inner conflict, and she does not allow the issues of others to become hers. In other words, if you are the Free Woman, you are not "entangled," which I will discuss in detail in the next chapter when I share with you concerning the Bondwoman.

The Free Woman is a forgiven woman, so Satan cannot hold her sins against her because Jesus has freed her from sin and the penalty of them too. If you are of this kind of woman, then your soul has been liberated by the gospel of Jesus Christ. You have sought to work out your salvation (deliverance and rescue) through your soul. I say simply to the Free Woman, *continue* to stay free, you are on your way to the promises of God being fulfilled in your life.

CHAPTER 18

The Bondwoman

But he who was of the bondwoman was born after the flesh.
—Galatians 4:23a

Our flesh (i.e. our fallen nature) is really a mess, and anything birthed out of it is not of God! There is no promise of God wrapped up in our flesh (again our fallen nature). All the promises of God are attached to a nature that is of God, and a born-again experience with Christ Jesus is what births a new nature in us.

Abram was given a promise of God that said he was going to make of him a great nation. This means that God had to give him a seed first for that seed to birth a nation, but after years of waiting, Abram and his wife Sarai had not had a baby, and they were getting older and impatient. So Genesis 16 shows us that Sarai got in her flesh and said (I'm paraphrasing), "I will fix this. I have a handmaiden by the name of Hagar, and she's an Egyptian, and I will command my husband to go sleep with her and get us a baby." Her husband Abram did not try to talk her out of this unholy plan, but instead, the Bible says he went in unto Hagar and she conceived. Abram was eighty-six when Ishmael was born. Let me pause a minute and tell you what Ishmael's name means in Hebrew; *God will hear*. This is such good news, woman, for this says even when we *mess up* and get in our flesh, God will hear us when we cry out to him. I will come back to this and show you this is scripture, that God hears us when we mess up and cry out to Him to deliver us from our own mess-ups in life, but *you have got to cry out to God, woman,* if you have messed up!

The word *Ishmael* or *Yishma'el*, which again means "God will hear," translates also to the Hebrew word *shama*, which is Strong's Number H8085 in the Strong's Concordance and means "to hear intelligently." This is all the more powerful because this implies to me that God can discern and hear intelligently when our cry is because our flesh has caused us to mess up. This means, woman, you don't have to hide your mess-ups in life from God. You don't have to let your mess-ups in life keep you bound or hold you captive for years. God is intelligent enough to perceive our mess-ups, so you might as well fess up and cry out for help, deliverance, and freedom from them. When you do, *God will hear* your cry right where you are (again, I will prove this to you before I end this chapter).

Now eventually, Sarai and Abram who is a hundred years old by now, conceived and birthed a baby named Isaac, and this baby is the seed of promise; Ishmael was not. Then that which he birthed out of the flesh (Ishmael) and the seed of promise (Isaac) are now trying to cohabitate in the same house, and it is not working, because that which was birthed out of the flesh is "mocking that which was birthed out of promise" (Genesis 21), so Sarah tells her husband to "cast out this bondwoman and her son: for the son of this bondwoman shall not be heir with my son, even with Isaac" (Genesis 21:10). In other words (again if I may paraphrase), Mother Sarah said, "I may have messed up by commanding you to go sleep with the bondwoman who was my handmaiden, but now I'm commanding that *you put her and her son out of our lives,* for they do not represent the promise that is on our life." Guess what? God backed up what Sarah (the Free Woman) said. Listen to what He said to Abraham:

> And God said unto Abraham, Let it not be grievous in thy sight because of the lad, and because of thy bondwoman; in all that Sarah hath said unto thee, *hearken unto her voice*; for in Isaac shall they seed be called. (Genesis 21:12; italics added)

75

Again, I say the promises of God are not wrapped up in nothing bound! You must be freed to enter the promises of God. The Bondwoman (Hagar) was an Egyptian slave. Sarah was the free woman! Likewise, woman, you need to be free to enter your promise, and you can't be enslaved to nothing if you are going to be a free woman.

So Abraham had to do as Sarah commanded. God told him, "You must hearken to your wife's voice."

Sidebar: God backs the voice of a free woman who is free indeed! I pray that insight is enough to make you desire to be a free woman and no longer a slave or a bondwoman to anything.

Now let's look at Hagar (the bondwoman) and her son, Ishmael, after they were cast out of Abraham and Sarah's house. She's now in the wilderness with only a loaf of bread and a bottle of water, with a teenager with a huge appetite to feed and take care of. She's now out of water and afraid that she and her child are going to die in the wilderness where, by the way, our messes of life can cause us to end up. Hagar begins to weep and cry out to God, but listen to what the scripture records in Genesis 21:17: "And God heard the voice of the lad." The Bible does not record what Ishmael said, but apparently, this teenager was sitting under a shrubbery saying something to God. He lifted his voice in some way, and again, *God heard him*, for the scriptures record that God heard the voice of the lad. That lad's name was Ishmael, whose name again means "and God will hear."

So in the end, God caused Hagar, Ishmael's mother, to open her eyes and see the well of provisions that God had. Likewise, will you see the well of provincial care, goodness, and mercy that God has for you, the Bondwoman, when you offer up your mess to the Lord and cry out for His mercy towards you. Truly, God cares for you, the Bondwoman, but He wants to see you free before He can progress you and lead you into the promises associated with a free life in Him.

Therefore, if you are a woman of this kind, cry out, bondwoman, for there is help for the mess you may currently find yourself in. I will be praying that the scales fall off your eyes now in Jesus's Name and that you no longer be bound, woman, by the messes of your past. Just as natural "messes" can be cleaned up, so can yours be cleaned up with a spiritual approach which the Father offers to you through His Son, Jesus. Don't believe it, just ask another woman whom you know is "now free," and more than likely, she will tell you she used to be *a hot mess* as well *but God helped her overcome*!

CHAPTER 19

The Desolate Woman

So Tamar remained desolate in her brother Absalom's house.
—2 Samuel 13:20

Desolation often follows abuse, violation, or an infringement of some kind. When the soul experiences the "effects" of these things (and there are many), there is a tendency to isolate oneself due to the fear of subsequent occurrences or the shame associated with the abuse, violation, or infringement. Physical abuse makes a person hide in secrecy of its occurrence or happening in one's life. Shame is horrible and affects your continence, so rather than appear to be shamed, many women *mask the shame* by either pretending to be happy or by simply becoming a Desolate Woman. This is exactly what happened to the biblical Tamar, David's daughter, after she was raped by her half-brother. Listen to the Scripture's depiction of Tamar's desolation:

> And Tamar put ashes on her head, and rent her garment of divers colours that was on her, and laid her hand on her head, and went on crying. And Absalom her brother said unto her, Hath Amnon thy brother been with thee? but hold now thy peace, my sister: he is thy brother; regard not this thing. So Tamar remained deso-

late in her brother Absalom's house. (2 Samuel
13:19–20)

I once lead a women's teaching session on this very subject entitled "The Violation of Tamar," for there are many Tamars in our
midst. I personally have never been "sexually violated;" however, I
have ministered to countless women who have been at the hands of
men, relatives, bosses, even pastors/spiritual leaders! Needless to say,
a violation of any kind is horrible, but a sexual violation or abuse of
any kind can leave lasting effects that will follow you for years if you
don't seek out help and counsel. I literally scream "No!" when I read
that Tamar's big brother told her, "Regard not this thing," which
contributed to Tamar's desolation. Anytime you allow someone to
tell you to *regard not* or give no attention to the violation or infringement or abuse that you have or are experiencing, you, woman, are
choosing (also) to disregard its effects on your own life! As a result,
you are imprisoning the soul of who you are in being into *desolation*!

What is *desolation*?

To be desolate means to be "laid to waste," barren and
"devastated"!

To be desolate also means to be lonely, solitary, deprived or des-
titute of inhabitants!

Desolation is a very dreary, gloomy, and dismal place where you
have feelings of abandonment by friends leaving you in a forlorn
place with *no hope!* This is a horrible place to abide.

Why would any woman want to be a desolate woman? If you
have no hope, you have nothing for your faith to rest upon. Not to
mention, my Bible tells me that "hope makes you *not ashamed!*" Your
hope is what will make you take off the mask that you are using to
cover up your shame. However, remember; there is no sign of hope in
a desolate place. You, woman, must come out of a place of desolation
and go to a place that offers you *a door of hope* coupled with safety,
and please know that Jesus is that door! God would love to use someone to lead or call you to such a place, for there is ministry for you
there. However, there is no ministry or service for you in a desolate
place.

Hear the scripture: "To whom God would make known what is the riches of the glory of this mystery among the Gentiles; which is Christ in you, the hope of glory" (Colossians 1:27). Please hear me on this: Christ (in you) is the hope that says, "There will be some level of glory or after this!"

Woman, I wish I could tell you that "bad, even horrible" things won't happen to you in this lifetime, but I can't. However, I can tell you that some level of glory will come out of what happened to you if you refuse to *be or become a desolate woman!* Again, I say there is no habitation in desolation, and you need not look for anyone to join you there. Again, I get so angry when I hear Absalom tell his sister to, in essence, "protect your abuser," "protect the pervert," and simply just disregard what was done to her. Are you kidding me? Sure, you should forgive those that violated you; however, for your soul's sake, you should not just act like nothing happened!

Therefore, I'm an advocate for counseling and support groups, even therapy, for victims of domestic abuse (all forms) and for victims of sexual assaults because these entities can aid and assist the victim to go from "victim to *victor*." All of these entities can help keep a woman out of desolation. With help, you will not feel abandoned and left alone and unsupported.

Woman, again, desolation is horrible, so please don't be the Desolate Woman! I don't care what happened to you; desolation is not your portion. Desolation can have graver effects on your soul than the act itself, so I leave you with this:

Don't allow any act of evil in this life drive you into desolation. Seek help! Seek support! Come to the altar of the Lord for prayer at your local church or ministry. Join a group for women who are victims of rape, domestic abuse, or incest! Call the Domestic Abuse hotline so you can get help during and after the abuse. Go to your pastor, a mother in the church, or a women's ministry leader (or the police even), just don't be the Desolate Woman!

Listed below are some hotline numbers to help you if this woman is you; if not, program these numbers in your phone in case another woman you may know needs them. Always run for shelter, not desolation. I will be praying for you!

- National Domestic Violence Hotline: 800-799-7233
- Mental Health Assistance: 877-816-1539
- 911 works still in case of an emergency.

CHAPTER 20

The Working Woman

This woman was full of good works and almsdeeds which she did.
—Acts 9:36

Some of your best "workers" are women. Whether they work in the home, the church, the field, the marketplace, or corporate America, women make for some awesome workers. I think we will all agree to this. Not to take away from men workers in any way who were fashioned by God to work and till the ground; however, the nature of a woman is "to help," and often "our help" is defined as some necessary work that a woman willingly does.

I applaud women who work jobs outside of the home, for I did it myself for many years. I know firsthand what it's like to work an eight-hour job and come home to cook, clean, help with homework while making sure your husband's needs are met, too, then wake up early the next morning and start the day (and the work) all over again. Whew! The problem occurs when the Working Woman does too much (which happens often) and fails to take care of herself physically, mentally, and emotionally. This is usually when the Working Woman sees a decline in her own health and or her own mental and emotional well-being; *not good, woman.* Here in the Bible we see such a woman. Her name is Dorcas by interpretation. Listen to Dorcas's story about how she worked so hard, got sick, and died!

> Now there was at Joppa a certain disciple named Tabitha, which by interpretation is called Dorcas: this woman was full of good works and almsdeeds which she did. And it came to pass in those days, that she was sick, and died: whom when they had washed, they laid her in an upper chamber. And forasmuch as Lydda was nigh to Joppa, and the disciples had heard that Peter was there, they sent unto him two men, desiring him that he would not delay to come to them. Then Peter arose and went with them. When he was come, they brought him into the upper chamber: and all the widows stood by him weeping, and shewing the coats and garments which Dorcas made, while she was with them. (Acts 9:36–39)

Dorcas was not only a working woman, but she was quite a charitable woman too, because the Bible said she was full of not just good works but also "almsdeeds," which means Dorcas was benevolent and quite compassionate in terms of meeting the needs of others. It also means that Dorcas did not get paid for everything she did, yet that did not stop her from working or doing charitable deeds for those in need.

Dorcas was a seamstress, and today, she would probably have her own clothing line too and would be deemed a fashion designer. The problem with this working woman is that she worked too hard and she allowed her good work to kill her. Dorcas was also probably a "workaholic" in modern terminology. If I was preaching from this passage of scripture, my thought would be: "Don't let your good works kill you!" The Working Woman needs "balance" and "self-care." Women (generally speaking) can have tendency to take care of everybody and everything else *before* or *without* taking care of themselves. Some working women even omit caring for themselves all together which, again, is not good. To the Working Woman, I say you cannot do it all. You must balance the scales of your life! Yes, your work brings great value to your company, the community, your church, your ministry, and certainly your family; however, if you work yourself into a grave, then all your work will cease. Therefore, I say to all the working women reading this chapter, please take time to rest, play or simply (smell the roses) while you can and please be diligent in taking care of yourself. Don't just make your husband's doctor appointment make one for yourself too. Don't just take your kids in for their annual physicals at the doctor get yours too. If you are of age; please be sure to get your mammogram and don't forget your Pap Smear too! You, The Working Woman must not overwork yourself and you must also tend to your well-being, too, as you see to the well-being of others!

Now let's go back to the Bible and let's look at this Biblical working woman named Dorcas. She was a Christian female or woman, as her name means. Tabitha or Dorcas in Greek also means "gazelle," and if you know anything about gazelles, *they can run fast*! According to Wikipedia, gazelles can run sixty miles per hour, and they can jump too. This was Dorcas, and the gazelle describes the nature of many working women. They can run all day and into the night too and can "jump" from one thing to the next quite easily without even resting or asking for help. I know some working women who can really burn the midnight oil; however, this is not me. Although I work diligently at home and in ministry, I realize the importance of rest, leisure time, play, and I get eight hours of sleep every night. Working women must learn this, for it is quite important to the longevity of your ability to continue to work without giving out, as my late mother-in-law, Lula Laws, would say.

Now I also believe that every working woman needs a "Peter" near her. Let me explain what I mean by this. When Dorcas died, the women were devastated, for apparently Dorcas had a women's clothing business and had made many outfits for these ladies. Now while Dorcas laid dead in the room upstairs, the widow women showcased her work, and they cried as they mourned her passing. We can say these women hated to see Dorcas leave them by way of death because they benefited so much from her good work. So when they heard Peter (an Apostle in the church) was near Joppa (their town), they sent two people to go and bring him where Dorcas lay dead. Bless

God, Peter (a man) came, and he put everybody out of the room, and notice what he did:

He prayed for her, which is something every working woman needs, especially if she's working in ministry or business. You, the Working Woman, need some man to cover and pray for you while you work. How awesome it is if you, the Working Woman, have a man, whether it's your husband, your father, a brother, or your pastor/apostle/bishop praying for you as you, woman, work. As Christian women, we typically are "praying women" ourselves; however, it is truly awesome to have a "praying man" beside you praying for you as you work. What a blessing!

Then Peter turned to Tabitha's body and told her to *get up*, as the CEB says; however, here's what else this man did when she "sat up." *He gave her "his hand" and he raised her up!* I found that to be so powerful and considerate. Perhaps Dorcas was still weak and having trouble getting up in strength. So Peter, the man of God, serving as the Apostle in this region, prayed for this very valuable working woman. He commanded her to arise, and he was considerate enough to give *her a helping hand!* Wow, I applaud this man of God and any man that lends some of "his strength" to the woman who is working and getting tired. I personally know this is the cry of many women, especially those who work in the home. "Can you (man) give me a hand of help with this housework, with these kids, etc." The misnomer is that working women don't need help, and that is a lie, even if she acts like she doesn't need help, *she does*. It is a falsity, woman, that you must not subscribe to, for it is this lie that is killing and exhausting women everywhere you find them working. Don't you dare not ask for help because asking for help may be the very thing that extends your life in the work force and in the earth.

Now let's look at what else this man named Peter did for Dorcas, whom he raised from the dead. Yes, he presented her alive to all the people she had done work for, but he did something else that's worth mentioning here. Hear the scripture: "Peter stayed for some time in Joppa with a certain tanner named Simon" (Acts 9:43).

The Bible told us at the beginning of this story that Tabitha (or Dorcas) was in Joppa, so instead of Peter going back to Lydda (which was a town near Joppa), he stayed for some time in Joppa. Sure, people believed in the Lord Jesus after this miracle was wrought by the Apostle Peter; however, something tells me that the man of God stayed for a season to make sure Dorcas remained well and did not overwork herself as the weaker vessel. How awesome is this! Truly, every working woman needs a caring "covering" man close by to ensure she does not overwork to her detriment, for the Working Woman is often *full* of good works, yet she must learn to pour out and work responsibly. Therefore, if you are a woman of this kind, please take time to rest and be *away* from your work. Go on vacation, and plan "staycations" too. Make sure you have a man covering you to pray and watch for your well-being. Lastly, to the Working Woman, I say remember the Sabbath Day and keep it holy, for when this day is observed, you will discover that the Lord of the Sabbath will work for you as you simply seek to observe Him and Him only.

CHAPTER 21

The Troubled Woman

And Jesus answered and said unto her, Martha, Martha,
thou art careful and troubled about many things
—Luke 10:41

It would be wrong to talk negatively about the Marthas of the church or home, for these women are some of your most willing *servants*. Where would our local churches be without Martha being in the midst? Martha's servitude makes things happen! Martha makes *serving* her business, no matter what is going on in her life, and although Martha is *relentless* in terms of her servitude, Martha is often so busy serving that she is not sitting and allowing the word of God to address her troubles nor her anxiety. In the church, Martha is the woman working in the kitchen or behind the scenes. In the workplace, Martha is the woman that's doing two or three jobs and picking up the slack wherever needed. Martha is usually not your preacher woman nor is she the woman sitting in the pew. Martha is that lady in the ministry who *always* has something to do during the worship service. Martha is the woman also who is too busy to *sit down* and get fed the word of God because, again, there is always something that needs to be done.

Surely, serving in the house is important, and someone must be "your servant," and yes, the Bible does tell us that the greatest among you is *your servant*. However, there must be a balance between serving and getting the word of God. Woman, you must realize that choosing to put the word of God as priority in your life is the good part, as Jesus ended up telling Martha, his friend, when she was fussing over the fact that her sister, Mary, was sitting and getting the word from Jesus rather than serving. When you don't get the word, you have nothing to use to address your troubles, and you will become anxious when trouble arises. Serving while troubled is a good way to serve with an attitude, short-tempered, even resentful. I have seen many mean servers in the church. They are far from pleasant and would do well to come away from serving a season to sit down and spend time at the feet of Jesus Christ (who is the word). Nothing can take the place of the word of God. Your troubles will respond to the Word, but if you don't have the Word in you, then you have nothing to counter your troubles with. You have nothing in you to serve your troubles, so they overwhelm you, and that's not a good state to serve in. The Bible says we are "to serve the Lord with gladness" (Psalms 100.2a), yet it's hard to be glad if you are bogged down with a bunch of troubles affecting our soul. Your troubles should not be anchoring your soul, but the word should be instead. The songwriter says, "My soul is anchored in the Lord" and Christ is His word.

When we look at the text that I opened this chapter with, Jesus was at the table being served by his troubled friend, Martha, and He could apparently tell she was troubled by her constant complaining. This is exactly what happens when you serve while troubled about "many things." So if this is you, woman (always complaining about something), you would do good to *sit down* and become a Mary by choosing to attend to the word of God instead of your "constant serving." The Marthas of today are quite busy and too busy to sit at the feet of Jesus, which is not good. Trouble is going to come our way for Job said in Job 14:1, "Man that is born of a woman is of few days and full of trouble." This means trouble is going to find you and it won't take long either. Trouble is going to make its way to you in some form, so you must learn early how to manage your troubles, and spending time in the word of God will help you do this. If you pay close attention to your pastor's Sunday morning messages, most of their sermons are usually trying to convey to you (in some way) how to deal with your problems or your troubles. You must know, woman, God is not afraid of a few troubles. God does not need to adjust Himself to handle your troubles. He is more than capable to handle your troubles, so why not position yourself in a place to get the word or the best part, the part that won't depart from you once you get it. Listen, woman, your troubles are going to come, then they are going to go. The word, on the other hand, is going to abide until it prospers in your life. So if you are the Troubled Woman, don't be afraid to take some time away from serving if you need to, and do spend a lot of time in the word and sitting under the preached word of God, because if you do, I guarantee you're going to hear something in the word that addresses your woes and your troubles. You can't go wrong with this decision either way.

THE CONCLUSION

You Are Not Every Woman

Thou shall also be a crown of glory in the hand of the Lord, and a royal diadem in the hand of the Lord.
—Isaiah 62:3

Hopefully by now you have seen the composite of the woman—good, bad, and ugly—and hopefully you have concluded with knowing that you are not every woman. The composite of the woman is her makeup or disparate or separate parts or elements. If you concluded from reading this book that there are some intricate parts of you or your womanhood that are not of God, as highlighted in this book, then you must ask yourself, where did that part of me come from? What caused the formulation of this part? It may be generational, it may be stemming from something you learned from your peers or from the culture of the world, it may be demonically influenced, it may have become a part of you after a negative experience in life.

If there are contributing factors to your make up as a woman that are evil or unholy or the like, then know this did not come by way of the hand of God, Elohim, your Creator. Woman, you must know that you were "fearfully and wonderfully made." You were made from the inside out! You are a "sculptured" woman of distinction that came into being at the hand of God. So you must be assured that if you became or have become "marred" in some way while in the hand of the Lord, do know He is likened unto a potter, as mentioned in Jeremiah 18:4, who is very capable of making you again *another vessel* as seemed good to the potter to make. Therefore, all you must do is be a woman who remains in rotation or on the potter's wheel. This is the wheel that can fix all defects by allowing you to simply be made again by Him. Truly, a personal relationship with the Lord Jesus Christ (the word) can do just that. The word of God renews your mind to who you are in Him. The Holy Spirit (a.k.a. The Spirit of Truth) will seek to remove all elements of falsity from your being if you simply heed His utterances. The word of God reminds you of whose you are, not just who you are. Staying in the word of God causes you to discover your "identity" in kind, so you will not tolerate being debased or devalued as a woman in godly kind.

Again, you're not Every Woman, but there is a variation in kind that you may see in you, and when you look at "your various kinds" or separated parts, you should also see a *predominate you*. However, the other parts of you which are disparate qualities do give credence to your distinction as a woman. Although you are not Every Woman (in kind), your distinction in kind can very well make you a multifaceted or multifunctional woman. For instance, you may be like me; a leading lady, with qualities that cause you to have great leadership, but you may also be the married woman who greatly understands submission in the home and can quickly and easily switch gears from *leader to wife*. If this is you, then it's unfair for someone who is unfamiliar with your kind as a woman to call you names that demean your capability to be a Leading Woman and a Married Woman. The aim of this book was to take you, the woman, on a journey to discover your distinction in kind, because the composite of The Woman is very vast. When God made The Woman, as mentioned in Genesis 2:22, from the rib of Adam (the first man), that was *ishsha* in Hebrew. Woman, or *ishsha*, is used in wide sense, according to the Strong's Concordance translation. When God made *ishsha*, or the woman, He made every female in distinction and kind. So just as we as parents are to train up a child in the way to go and in accordance with their special bent—meaning his or her "abilities or talents," which can vary from child to child even in the same family—likewise, are not all women the same in kind. For the composite of who we were made to be (at the hand of God) varies from woman to woman. Therefore, you as a woman need to know and recognize your kind in distinction. You need to realize that you have separate parts of you as a woman, and each part has a special ability or quality attached to it. There is a part of you that can make you a worshipping woman, then there is another part of you that can make you the virtuous woman, then there could be a part of you that causes you to be The Blessed And Highly Favored Woman. I pray you can now see this, woman, in kind.

Then, conversely, there could be a contributing part of you that makes you the strange woman in kind. Here's where you must ask yourself, "Who added this part to me?" I can assure you, woman, *it was not God*. Again, you may have had a negative experience in life that "added a part" to you that is not of God. If that is the case, you, woman, must get delivered of all parts that pervert you as a woman in kind. Understand this; a perverted part can negatively affect the whole (you). May you be loosed and delivered from false perceptions of you, The Woman that is fearfully and wonderfully made by God!

Now I'm thankful that I'm not Every Woman, but I am the woman who God designed and sculpted me to be, and I make no apologies for this! I am a Purposeful Woman who lives every day being purpose driven in work and in my living. This causes me to be a Victorious Woman who manages (through the grace of God) to overcome every evil attack on my life through Christ Jesus. Therefore, woman, don't seek to be every woman, and don't allow anyone or anything nor any negative experience in life to make you a False Woman all out of sorts with God's will for your life, and I pray that this book highlighting the composite of the woman in kind chapter by chapter, sentence by sentence, has caused you to find you, or at least has provoked you to be a better woman in kind.

ABOUT THE AUTHOR

Dr. Sharon Peters has been preaching and teaching the gospel of Jesus Christ for twenty years and has lived a good life in HD for over thirty years as a saved woman of God. As a set gift in the church and as an affirmed Apostle, she works to edify, strengthen, and grow to maturity the disciples of Christ through her teaching and ministry of "strong meat," which challenges and fosters growth and development if applied. Apostle Sharon (as she is affectionately called by the church) received her Doctor of Divinity degree in 2012 from the Calvary School of Ministry for Independent Biblical Studies (an affiliate of Grace Theological Seminary of Loris, South Carolina). In 2015, she earned her Doctor of Theology Degree from Open Arms International Bible College and Seminary School of Chicago, Illinois. In 2018, she received her Doctor of Philosophy Degree in Biblical Studies from Empowerment Theological Institution & Seminary.

Apostle Sharon has great love for the "study of the Holy Scriptures," and truly she is a workman who is not ashamed because she is proficient in rightly dividing the word of truth. She is an apostolic woman who is given to the ministry of the word and prayer in accordance with Acts 6:4. As a result of her intense studies, coupled with her early morning communing with the Holy Spirit who leads her into the deep, she has become a noted teacher who can reveal new truths and uncover mysteries hidden in the Word of God. Her greatest passion, however, is her love for women's ministry; and she is called upon to minister to women everywhere. She is known for her caring and compassionate ministry to women. Through her signature ministry, Sweet Rose of Sharon Women's Ministry (SRS), which she founded in 2002 and in which she still currently serves as president, she has hosted many conferences, seminars, retreats, and banquets, drawing women from all walks of life. Dr. Sharon Peters has been used by God to deliver many messages to women and write and publish several books with the woman in mind like *Help for the Help Meet, Thoughts of the Morning, 31 Days of Divine Thinking, Teach Me to Pray*, and others.

Truly, she is a woman called for such a time as this and is definitely being used by God to bring healing, deliverance, and restoration to THE WOMAN.